T0047099

WICCA
NATURE MAGIC

A BEGINNER'S GUIDE TO
WORKING WITH NATURE SPELLCRAFT

LISA CHAMBERLAIN

STERLING ETHOS
New York

STERLING ETHOS
New York

An Imprint of Sterling Publishing Co., Inc.

STERLING ETHOS and the distinctive Sterling Ethos logo
are registered trademarks of Sterling Publishing Co., Inc.

Text © 2019, 2022 Lisa Chamberlain

All rights reserved. No part of this publication may be reproduced, stored
in a retrieval system, or transmitted in any form or by any means
(including electronic, mechanical, photocopying, recording, or otherwise)
without prior written permission from the publisher.

Portions of this book were originally published as *Wicca Tree Magic*
in 2019 by Chamberlain Publications

This publication includes alternative therapies that have not been scientifically tested,
is intended for informational purposes only, and is not intended to provide or replace
conventional medical advice, treatment or diagnosis or be a substitute to consulting
with licensed medical or health-care providers. The publisher does not claim or
guarantee any benefits, healing, cure or any results in any respect and shall not be
liable or responsible for any use or application of any content in this publication in any
respect including without limitation any adverse effects, consequence, loss or damage
of any type resulting or arising from, directly or indirectly, any use or application of any
content herein. All trademarks are the property of their respective owners, are used
for editorial purposes only, and the publisher makes no claim of ownership and shall
acquire no right, title, or interest in such trademarks by virtue of this publication.

ISBN 978-1-4549-4108-8
ISBN 978-1-4549-4107-1 (e-book)

For information about custom editions, special sales, and premium purchases,
please contact specialsales@unionsquareandco.com.

Printed in Canada

2 4 6 8 10 9 7 5 3 1

unionsquareandco.com

Cover design: *front*, Elizabeth Lindy; *back*, Igor Satanovsky
Interior design by Christine Heun and Sharon Leigh Jacobs

Cover art: Depositphotos.com: NadezhdaSh (pendant); Shutterstock.com: Croisy
(trinity knot); Epine (leaves, acorn); Morphart Creation (bird)

traditions. Part 2 offers profiles of common magical trees and flowers, including their energetic properties, magical uses, and associated folklore. You'll also find advice for forging and deepening a personal connection with the spiritual energy of the natural world around you.

Part 3 offers a collection of spells, meditations, rituals, and recipes for working with the magic of Nature.

May you find knowledge, guidance, insight, and inspiration for your journey in the pages that follow.

Blessed be.

INTRODUCTION

ANYONE WHO HAS EVER HAD THE GOOD FORTUNE TO FIND themself standing in a forest can attest to the peaceful, almost otherworldly feeling of *watching* tall branches sway in the breeze and the flickering of sunlight through a canopy of bright green leaves. For Witches, the forest is a place to commune with the unseen creative forces of the Universe. The same is true of fields, mountains, deserts, oceans, and canyons—any place where the energies of Nature still prevail over the destructive tendencies of human beings can be a place of communion. All that's needed for a magical experience is to tune in to Nature's silent, graceful presence.

Of course, not everyone can go for a nature hike, let alone hold a ritual in a forest. But magical energy can be felt wherever trees, plants, animals, and even rocks reside, whether it's a national park or your own backyard. Even if you live in a high-rise in the city, you can still make a point of connecting in person with the energies of Nature by taking a walk in a local park or growing flowering plants on your windowsill. The aim of this guide is to encourage you to cultivate a relationship with the magic of Nature in your own individual way, get hands-on practical experience working with trees and flowers, and deepen your spiritual practice in harmony with the Earth.

In part 1, we'll explore the magical significance of trees, flowers, and nature spirits to our pagan ancestors, as well as to the contemporary practice of Wicca, which draws on those older

PART THREE

NATURE RITUALS, SPELLS, AND CRAFTS

A GRIMOIRE FOR THE GREAT OUTDOORS.........................107

ENCHANTED FOREST MEDITATION................................108

HARVESTING FROM TREES FOR MAGICAL WORK.............111

A RITUAL FOR HARMLESS HARVESTING 113

TREE TRUNK GROUNDING RITUAL................................115

GREEN MAN/WOMAN LEAF CROWN..............................117

WAND CRAFTING..121

TREE INCENSE 123

AUTUMN HARVEST EASY ABUNDANCE SPELL................124

WARM HEALTHY WINTER HEARTH SPELL.....................126

"BUILD YOUR OWN" PROTECTION WITCH JAR 128

SPELL FOR WELCOMING LOVE INTO YOUR HOME...........130

"BACK TO NATURE" SPIRIT CHARM............................132

CONCLUSION..134

ACKNOWLEDGMENTS...137

SUGGESTIONS FOR FURTHER READING...........................139

PICTURE CREDITS..141

INDEX...143

ABOUT THE AUTHOR..150

PART TWO

TREES, FLOWERS, AND NATURE SPIRITS

NATURE'S MAGICAL INHABITANTS 53

THIRTEEN MAGICAL TREES 54

    Ash 56

    Birch 59

    Cedar 61

    Elm 64

    Fir.. 66

    Hawthorn 69

    Holly 72

    Maple 74

    Oak 77

    Pine.. 80

    Rowan (Mountain Ash) 82

    Willow 85

    Yew 88

GATHERING AND GROWING MAGICAL FLOWERS 91

MAGICAL ASSOCIATIONS FOR COMMON WILDFLOWERS 95

CONNECTING WITH NATURE SPIRITS 100

BRANCHING OUT 103

CONTENTS

INTRODUCTION viii

PART ONE

THE SPIRIT OF NATURE

ANIMISM AND MAGIC 3

TREES AND THE "OLD RELIGION" 6

NORTHERN EUROPEAN TREE WORSHIP 10

   The Druids and Celtic Magic 10

   Trees and the Ancient Germans 17

TREES IN WICCAN COSMOLOGY 23

   The Oak King and the Holly King 24

   The Green Man (and Green Woman) 26

   The Wheel and the Elements 28

   Trees and Tools of the Craft 30

      The Wand 31

      The Broom 35

      The Bonfire 35

THE MAGICAL ENERGY OF FLOWERS 40

   Flower Folk Magic 42

NATURE SPIRITS: ELEMENTALS AND THE GENIUS LOCI 45

GETTING UP CLOSE AND PERSONAL 49

FOR LILY

who arrived right on time

PART ONE

THE SPIRIT OF NATURE

ANIMISM AND MAGIC

IF YOU HAVE EVER SPENT QUALITY TIME IN THE WILDS OF Nature—a forest, a desert, a beach, a mountain range—you've likely felt an energy there that isn't perceived in the urban landscapes of the human-occupied world. Whether you experience this energy as soothing, awe-inspiring, or maybe even intimidating, it's palpable from the moment you step into the landscape, and it often lingers in your mind for a while after you leave.

Each natural area on Earth has its own signature energy and has a magnetic pull on those who love to spend time there. As Witches know, experiencing Nature goes beyond simply seeing its inherent beauty with your eyes or listening to the sounds of animals, waves, or wind. It's also about how you *feel* when you're in Nature, which can be harder to describe than what you perceive with your five ordinary senses. That feeling is an indication that you're picking up on the energy of the land or water all around you, the eternal yet dynamic energy of the Earth that our ancestors also felt and is always available for us to tune in to.

Unlike in modern societies, which have created boundaries between the "wilderness" and the "civilized world," the earliest humans lived their lives at one with the energies of Nature. Their experience of these energies was at the root of the earliest known spiritual belief systems, which are referred to by modern anthropologists as "animism." Animism is a worldview that sees absolutely no separation between the material world and the spiritual world. Animistic qualities are at work in many religious belief systems around the world, especially in African, Native American, and Southeast Asian cultures. Animism was certainly present in pre-Christian Europe as well, as can be seen in the mythological lore of ancient Germanic and Celtic tribes.

What animism looks like in practice varies across cultures, but two broad strands of belief are relevant to this guide. The first is the belief that there is a soul, or spirit, in inanimate objects found in Nature, such as trees, mountains, rocks, rivers, lakes, plants, and so on, as well as animals. In some animistic cultures, this "soul" is recognized in some material things but not necessarily others. For example, there might be one particular tree in a grove that is considered sacred, while others around it are not. This doesn't mean that the other trees are seen as separate from the spirit world, only that they don't possess the same kind of potent spiritual energy that humans are able to recognize and interact with. The second strand is the belief in an unseen force that organizes and powers the material world. The focus here is not on individual objects, but on the organizing principle of the big picture. In this view, everything is interconnected, and all things are imbued with spirit because they were created by spiritual forces. Both of these ideas—the interconnectedness of all things and the spiritual energies inherent in natural phenomena—are at the heart of what makes magic possible.

Wiccans and other Witches, especially those who follow the paths of green and hedge witchery, are animists who work with the energies of Nature. They understand trees, flowers, plants, and animals to be individual expressions of the Universe, each with its own spiritual energy. This is also true, of course, of crystals and other stones, bodies of water, and anything else found in Nature. Witches also recognize nonphysical spiritual expressions

of this universal energy, such as the Elements of Earth, Air, Fire, and Water. Some might communicate with spirit-plane beings, often referred to as "faeries," which are imperceptible through ordinary human senses. Others might simply recognize and appreciate a more general, less definable spiritual presence while communing with Nature. Whatever the case, tuning in to natural energy is itself an act of magic and a good way to increase your connection to your own magical power. So is learning about the specific energies of the trees, flowers, and other plant life in your environment, as well as the magical correspondences and folklore of these plant beings.

In the following pages, we'll explore the history of the spiritual relationships between trees and our European pagan ancestors, which fostered magical traditions that are still followed to this day. We'll examine the significance of trees in Wiccan belief and practice, from our concepts of deity to the use of time-honored magical tools. We'll also take a look at the history and practice of flower magic, and the mysterious realm of nature spirits.

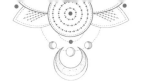

TREES AND THE "OLD RELIGION"

WE ALL KNOW THAT HUMANS, AS WELL AS ANIMALS, plants, and insects, depend heavily on trees for basic survival. Trees provide food for a whole host of living things, both visible and invisible, and shelter for humans and animals alike. As our earliest ancestors evolved, trees became the chief source of fuel for fire, thus providing a crucial turning point toward civilization. And before people began to build their own permanent shelters, trees often served as the only available cover from pelting rain and the fierce heat of the sun. They were also beneficial to our health and general well-being; the bark, leaves, berries, and sap of many trees were used for medicine and healing, while fruits and nuts provided sustenance. Twigs, branches, and stumps were transformed into tools and carved into toys for children.

The magical and spiritual significance of trees was also recognized by our animist forebears all around the world. Myth and lore surrounding trees is found in every land inhabited by humans, from the Inuits of the Arctic to the Akha mountain people of southeast Asia to the San people of the Kalahari Desert in southern Africa. Beliefs about the nature and purpose of trees vary as widely as the cultures that have traditionally revered them, and many of these ancient beliefs are still alive today in some form. For example, in some cultures, trees are believed to have their own unique souls. In others, trees are merely homes for spirits, who can choose to inhabit them or leave them at any time. The ancient Greeks and Romans, however, believed that hamadryads (tree-dwelling nature

spirits) would die
when their trees did,
whether the tree was
cut down or died of
natural causes.

Tree spirits might be
nonhuman in origin, such
as faeries, dryads, and
other Elemental beings,
or they might be the
actual ancestors of
the people who live
near them. Several
belief systems allow
for deceased humans
to come into their next incarnation as trees. And in many tales
from ancient Greece, the gods could turn humans into trees. Trees
could also be the homes of deities and were often associated with
particular ones. For example, there is a grove in India considered
sacred to the monkey god Hanuman. For the ancient Romans, oak
trees were connected with Jupiter, the god of the sky, and a special
fig tree in the center of Rome was sacred to Romulus, the city's
mythical founder. Trees were the first temples in the religious
life of many peoples, including the Greeks, the Celts, and other
ancient Europeans.

Some cultures believed that trees can feel pain, and certain
trees have been said to make terrible sounds when being cut down.
The ancient Persians waited until trees fell naturally on their own,
rather than causing them such distress. Other societies would
ask for forgiveness, make substantial offerings to the tree before
felling it, or consult with the community's shaman to determine
whether the tree would come down willingly. The Celts believed

that permission must be sought from an elder tree before cutting it down, and even then many people were still wary of doing so.

These traditions were often about more than just respect for the trees as sovereign beings—people also feared that the spirits of the tree would be angered and take revenge. Indeed, trees were not universally viewed as benevolent or harmless beings. Forests, which were unfathomably vast in many parts of the world before the onset of human modernization, show up in many myths and folktales as intimidating, dangerous, and forbidden places where evil spirits reside and unsuspecting wanderers could disappear forever.

Despite this trepidation about forests, the value of trees to human survival was widely acknowledged by ancients around the globe. Trees stood as symbols of life, abundance, fertility, and renewal. Many belief systems include a version of the archetypal Tree of Life, including Judaism and (by association)

Christianity, and artifacts depicting similar iconography are found in ancient Iran and Mesopotamia, China, and several European cultures. These depictions often feature a lush, abundant tree with many fruits, surrounded by animals. In some myths, the tree of life is literally the origin of all plant life—it was the first living plant on Earth and contains the seeds of all other plants to come.

Trees are also associated with knowledge and wisdom, such as the Bodhi tree under which the Buddha became enlightened. It is perhaps this association with wisdom that gave rise to the Kabbalah, a mystical tradition that began in Judaism and has been adapted over the centuries by both Christians and magical practitioners alike. Visually depicted in the shape of the Tree of Life, the Kabbalah is a framework for viewing the transformation of nonphysical reality into the physical reality of the world as we know it. All of creation is represented within the "branches" of the Tree of Life, and many Witches who work with this symbolic system find that their spiritual and magical practice is enhanced by studying the Tree of Life through the lens of the Western mystery tradition.

Another common archetypal symbol is the World Tree, which connects the heavens and the earth. In many cultures, trees are integral parts of creation myths, and they are often seen as ladders or bridges between the physical world of human beings and the invisible world of the gods. It has been theorized that this universal pattern could stem from ancient genetic memory, an acknowledgment of our earliest history as tree-dwellers, when the forest could indeed have been the whole world. The World Tree archetype appears in belief systems from Siberia to the native tribes of North America, as well as in Chinese, Hindu, and African traditions. Some people equate the World Tree with the Tree of Life, but while they may be interchangeable in some cosmologies, in others there is a distinct difference. The Tree of Life is a symbol of what living organisms need to survive and thrive, while the World Tree relates to everything in the Universe—the gods, spirit beings, and geographical features like mountains and rivers. The World Tree is, in many cases, the Universe itself.

NORTHERN EUROPEAN
TREE WORSHIP

IN THE NORTHERN EUROPEAN WORLD, WHERE MANY OF OUR neo-pagan traditions come from, two ancient cultures in particular are known for working with trees as a means of connecting with the divine and the magical energies present throughout the Universe: the Celts and the ancient Germanic peoples. Since the legends, myths, and lore of both of these cultural groups was primarily oral rather than written down, much of the information we have about their beliefs and activities comes from outside observers, such as the ancient Roman writers Tacitus and Pliny. We also have plenty of mythology that was finally written down in later centuries, but because many of these later sources were imbued with the influence of Christianity, it's hard to know just how accurate the details of the stories are. However, we can still glean plenty of insight into how our pagan ancestors worked with the natural wisdom of the trees that grew in their native lands.

The Druids and Celtic Magic

The Celts were an ethnolinguistic group of tribes who originated in central Europe and migrated to several places on the continent and throughout the British Isles. The Druids were their spiritual and philosophical leaders, who held authority over the religious rites, education, legal matters, healing, and the oral tradition of

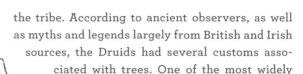

the tribe. According to ancient observers, as well as myths and legends largely from British and Irish sources, the Druids had several customs associated with trees. One of the most widely known is their reverence for oaks and in particular oak groves, which the Druid priests considered sacred and where they held religious rites. The word *druid* has actually been connected to an old Welsh name for oak, and translated as "knowing the oak tree." The Druids were also most certainly magicians—so much so that even in recent Irish history, the words *Druid* and *magician* meant the same thing.

One of the most well-known Druidic rituals involved the harvesting of mistletoe from a sacred oak. Using a sickle, the Druids would climb the tree on the sixth day of the lunar cycle and slice a branch of mistletoe so that it fell onto a white cloak placed on the ground beneath the tree. This harvesting ritual was followed by the sacrifice of two white bulls and then a feast. The purpose of this practice is unclear (as is the specific role of the mistletoe), but it is a fair assumption that the bulls were offered to one or more of the gods in the ancient Celtic pantheon. Druids were said to revere mistletoe because it "fell" from the realm of the gods, and this marked the oak tree on which it grew as sacred. Mistletoe was also associated with healing powers (and has in fact been used recently as a part of treatment for cancer patients). White is said to have represented purity to the Druids, which may shed light on the use of white bulls and a white cloth, as well as another reason for the importance of mistletoe—its white berries.

Although the oak is perhaps the tree most widely associated with the Druids, it is definitely not the only one they worked with. It seems the Celts believed that all trees have spirits, and that those trees with the most palpable magical energy were inhabited by the most powerful spirits. Furthermore, each species of tree held its own type of spirit, and so one species of tree could be more suitable than another for a particular magical purpose. These spirits would have been present in all of the trees mentioned in connection with the Druids, including rowan, hazel, yew, aspen, birch, and apple. Branches, boughs, and bark from these and other trees might be used for healing, divination, wand making, and/or various rituals. For example, leafy birch branches were used to cover the body of the deceased as it was carried to the grave on a wooden pallet. The grave itself was measured with a rod of aspen or yew, which was inscribed with Ogham lettering (though it is unclear what the inscription may have meant).

Ogham (pronounced *OH-um*) is the name of the script, or alphabet, used for writing the Irish language during the first few centuries of the Common Era (CE). Some historians assert that the alphabet was actually developed within the first century BCE or earlier, but it's hard to know since any inscriptions made on wood would have disintegrated well before Ogham was studied by scholars. It is believed that the Druids invented this alphabet, possibly as a means of communicating in secret, so that the authorities in neighboring Roman-ruled Britain would not understand them.

Several of the letters in Ogham were named for trees—birch, alder, willow, oak, and hazel. Additionally, the ancient Irish words for letters were *feda* (trees) and *nin* (forking branches), appropriate names for the branch-like shapes of the letters themselves. Some people believe that Ogham was also a system of magical symbols and a form of divination that only initiated Druids had access to. This belief has never been proven academically, but it has nevertheless inspired the practices of many modern Celtic-oriented Witches and other pagans.

We do know that the Druids used actual trees in a variety of divination methods.

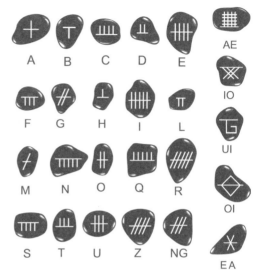

OGHAM ALPHABET

In one, the future was divined from the appearance of the roots of trees. In another, branches were fashioned into "omen sticks." These were cast upon the ground, and answers were extrapolated from the way they landed. (From some tales in Irish mythology, it appears that Ogham lettering may have been involved in this method, but it's unclear how the symbols would have been interpreted.) In a more elaborate divination ritual, the hides of the sacrificial bulls mentioned on page 11 were spread over a frame made from a rowan tree, with the inside of the hide facing upward, and then read for signs of upcoming events.

Wands were clearly of great significance to the Druids, who carried them in part as a signifier of their position within Celtic society. Their more important function, however, was to direct energy toward a desired result, much as they are used in Wiccan and other pagan ritual and magic today. It is also thought that Druids spoke special words, or "charms," while using the wand for magical work. Wands were made from the branches of trees, and wands made from hazel, rowan, elder, apple, and yew appear in Irish mythology as well as in Celtic folk customs, which most likely trace back to the pre-Christian days of the Druids. In the myths, wands are used for transformation—usually of a person or deity into an animal—as well as divination and defense.

In the folk traditions, some of which are still followed today, wands of hazel and rowan were used to bless and protect the home, often as part of cross-quarter day celebrations (like Beltane and Samhain). On Imbolc, or Saint Brigid's Day in Ireland, a wand made of willow or birch was left for the goddess-turned-saint Brigid, in hopes that she would visit the household in the night.

Irish lore sheds light on many other magical traditions surrounding trees. Hawthorn blossoms were considered unlucky if brought into the house, and Beltane Eve was the only time when hawthorn branches could be harvested safely, without risking misfortune. Beltane was also a good time to harvest hazel branches for wands, as they would then have more powerful potential, particularly for protection from evil spirits. A wand of elder also had protective properties and was associated with the faerie folk. Hazel wands were used for weather magic and for divining the location of water.

The fruits and nuts of sacred trees were also important in Irish myths, legends, and customs. Hazelnuts were used magically for knowledge and wisdom, and Scottish Druids were known to chew on hazelnuts on Samhain to gain prophecies about the future from the Otherworld. Acorns were eaten by the Druids of Gaul for similar purposes. Apples are central to some of the most well-known magical traditions from the Celtic world, which is where the Halloween tradition of bobbing for apples originates. The game was played by young unmarried people as a fun kind of marriage divination—the first person to grab hold of an apple with their teeth would be the next one in the community to marry. Another love divination ritual called for peeling an apple in one long strip and tossing the peel to the floor; if it fell in the shape of a letter, it would indicate the first initial of a future lover's name.

Some of these beliefs and customs continue among Celtic people today. For example, it is still believed by many that faeries dwell in any place where oak, ash, and thorn trees grow together. And "wishing trees" are still in use throughout the Celtic Isles. The most well-known type of wishing trees is found growing near certain wells that are considered sacred (or "holy"). Their branches are hung with strips of cloth, which represent the prayers, petitions, or magical intentions of people who tie them. These trees are traditionally whitethorn, hawthorn, or ash trees, but the tree's proximity to the well is more important than its species. The chief purposes of these wishing tree rituals are to facilitate healing and fertility, though some people may tie a cloth simply to honor the spirit (or saint, for Christians) of the well. Another type of wishing tree is a "coin tree": typically an oak, ash, or hawthorn tree that has fallen down and whose trunks and branches are studded with coins. People press the coins into the wood for all kinds of wishes. Wishing tree traditions are practiced in many other regions across the globe—from Asia to South America.

But local descendants of the Celts are not the only people who keep the ancient tree traditions alive. Modern Druids (or Neo-Druids), Witches, and other pagans living in many places around the world have drawn substantially on Celtic myth and lore to shape their magical practices. Today's Neo-Druids, for example, may employ a wand made from an apple branch, hung with small bells in the manner of their Druid ancestors, to access the Otherworld and invite friendly spirits to join in. And many modern groups of Druids are known as groves, whether they meet among the trees or in a member's living room.

Ogham also continues to be significant for magical practitioners who find meaning in its symbols and its association with sacred trees. Much of the modern lore about Ogham originates with a book published in the mid-twentieth century called *The White Goddess*, by poet Robert Graves, who suggested that the symbolic system encoded ancient esoteric wisdom that had been handed down over the centuries, ultimately arriving in the hands of Irish Druids.

Based on earlier works by Celtic scholars, as well as local folklore surrounding the trees and other plants the Ogham letters were named for, Graves and others devised a system of magical and divinatory meanings for Ogham that are still used today. Graves is also largely responsible for the invention of the Celtic tree calendar, a thirteen-month calendar that begins with the Winter Solstice and has twenty-eight days per month. Each month is named for a tree, beginning with Beith (birch) and ending with Ruis (elder).

Much of Graves's work has since been discredited by contemporary scholars, and reconstructionist Celtic pagans generally dismiss the practices that were inspired by his theories. Nonetheless, elements of Graves's unique, imaginative work have had a substantial influence on many forms of modern paganism—including Wicca—and are still relevant today. The same is true, of course, of the authentic lore and traditions of the Celts, particularly when it comes to working with the magic of trees.

Trees and the Ancient Germans

The diverse tribes collectively known as the ancient Germanic peoples, who migrated throughout the central, western, and northern areas of Europe (including much of England and parts of Ireland and Scotland), are also believed to have centered much of their religious activity around trees. Their Roman observers noted that their religious rituals took place in groves rather than in temples, and that both groves and individual trees were often dedicated to a particular deity. Some contemporary scholars believe that the woods were indeed the first temples of the ancient Germans, and that built structures designated for ritual purposes didn't come along until later. Whatever the case, the religious significance of trees was clearly part of Northern European culture until well into the second millennium CE, as the Christian church found itself having to ban certain trees due to their association with pagan ritual. In fact, the role trees played in the lives of these pagan ancestors has had a lasting influence on Western culture, which can still be detected in both Christian and secular holiday traditions today.

Much of what we know about the beliefs of the Germanic peoples comes from Norse mythology and literature. It's here that we find one of the most well-known versions of the World Tree, known as Yggdrasil. This great tree stands at the center of the Universe, and the nine worlds of the Norse cosmology are held within its roots, trunk, and branches. All things within the Universe are connected to one another through the vast expanse of this tree. Animals, humans, mythical creatures, and gods all benefit from Yggdrasil in one way or another, as the tree runs through all the dimensions in which they dwell. Mythical creatures live within the tree, and the gods assemble there to discuss important events and watch over the worlds.

Yggdrasil is particularly associated with the concept of fate and with a kind of shamanic journeying. The Norns, the mythical female beings said to weave the world's past, present, and future, reside at the base of the World Tree and tend to its roots. Odin, the god who discovered the secrets of the magical symbols known as runes, gained this knowledge by hanging upside down from a branch of Yggdrasil for nine days and nights, until he grasped their hidden meanings. These and other stories within Norse mythology show how trees were viewed as intermediaries between the world of humans and the spirit worlds.

Traditionally, the World Tree has been believed to be an ash tree, and it is translated as such in all of the myths in which it appears. However, many scholars have reason to believe that Yggdrasil is actually a yew tree, and that *ash* was a mistranslation of the old myths. For one thing, Yggdrasil is described as being an everlasting and evergreen tree. Yet the ash tree is not an evergreen, nor does it live exceptionally long (most species live one hundred to two hundred years). By contrast, the yew is a conifer, staying green all year round, and can live well over one thousand years. Furthermore, in many parts of Northern Europe, the yew has traditionally represented the Yule tree (perhaps because of its association with death and regeneration), which is seen as a symbol of Yggdrasil.

The yew is relatively modest in size, however, in comparison to the mighty ash, which can grow to heights over 100 feet (30.5 m), compared to the yew's typical height of 30 to 60 feet (9–18 m). This may partly explain why the ash was assumed to be the model for Yggdrasil. At any rate, the ash was clearly important to the Norse, as the first man was said to be created from this tree. (The first woman was created from either an elm tree, a rowan tree, or a vine, depending on the translation from Old Norse.) Several other sacred trees are mentioned in Norse mythology as well, including Barnstokkr, which a king's hall was built around, and Glasir, which stands in the front of Valhalla, the hall where fallen warriors are welcomed into the afterlife.

Like the Druids, the ancient Norse made use of wands for ritual and magical purposes. However, the carrier of the wand in this case was typically a woman, known as a *völva*, or seeress. The *völur* (plural of *völva*) held an elevated place in Norse society and would never be harmed while walking about, for they knew powerful magic and were respected and valued (as well as somewhat feared) by their communities. In Norse mythology, even Odin, the Allfather, consults a *völva* about the future. *Völva* translates as *staff carrier*, which points to the significance of the wand (a shortened version of the staff) as part of the seeress's function. She is said to sit on a special raised platform, holding her staff, and with the aid of song enter a trance, through which she then gains information from the spirit world. Scholars believe the staff was considered a physical manifestation of the World Tree, serving to link the visible human world with the spirit realms. Compared to what we know of the Celts, there is less evidence within Norse literature that certain types of trees were used for specific forms of magic, and the wands and staffs found among archeological discoveries from this time period are typically made of iron and bronze. However, wooden staffs have also been discovered in the graves of

seeresses. As with the Druids, we can assume that wooden wands were in wide use among the Norse magicians, but the evidence has decayed over the centuries.

Like the Irish and their Ogham, the ancient Germanics also had a system for writing that was related both to magic and to trees. The first Germanic alphabet, known as the Elder Futhark, was developed sometime around the first century CE, and several newer alphabets evolved from the Elder Futhark over time, as the Germanic languages diversified due to widespread migration. The symbols that made up these various related alphabets are known collectively as the runes. While some of these symbols were adapted from other nearby cultures (most likely in northern Italy) many had already existed as powerful magical symbols among the Germanic tribes. These symbols had been used in magical workings, possibly for thousands of years. By carving the symbols into objects made from stone, bone, metal, and—of course—wood, a rune master could change the course of unfolding events.

Several rune names in these symbolic systems correspond to specific sacred trees. For example, the rune called Ansuz in the Elder Futhark system is associated with the ash tree. Another rune, Eihwaz, literally translates to *yew*. Berkanan is translated both as *birch tree* and *birch goddess*. In the Anglo-Saxon rune system, Ansuz evolved into the runes Asec, meaning ash, and Ac, which translates to *oak tree*. The rune Yr stands for a bow made from the branch of a yew tree. The magical energies of these trees were part of what imbued these specific symbols with their power. Even the word *rune* is associated with a magical tree—the Old Norse word *runa* is the root word for *rowan*, which is sacred to both the Celts and the Norse and is known in some places as the "rune tree."

Runes were also used in divination, according to the Roman writer Tacitus. The diviners would harvest a branch from a fruit-bearing tree, cut it into strips, and carve a symbol on each one. A white cloth was laid upon the ground, and the carved strips of wood were scattered upon it. The rune reader would look up toward the sky to ask the gods for their assistance before choosing three of the symbols at random. These three were then interpreted for information about the question being asked.

Runic symbols are still used in forms of magic and divination today by modern practitioners of reconstructed Norse traditions, such as Asatru and Heathenism, as well as by some eclectic Wiccans and other Witches. The runes' individual meanings and divinatory interpretations are derived from both historical sources and intuitive associations. For example, Ansuz (ash), named for the tree on which Odin is said to have hung in order to obtain the secrets of the runes, is often interpreted to indicate messages from the higher realms. Ansuz is used in magic today to gain wisdom in confusing situations and to communicate with the divine. Eiwhaz (yew) is associated with death and regeneration. In magic, this rune is a strong symbol of protection, banishing, and spiritual development.

Berkanan (birch) signifies new beginnings and growth. It is used in magic for fertility, creativity, and strengthening family ties. One of the better-known Germanic magical practices is the creation of a runic talisman by carving runes appropriate to the purpose into a piece of wood or other natural material. Traditionally, this tine, as it is called, is made from a branch harvested from a live tree, after securing the tree's permission.

Tree-related customs handed down from the Germanic peoples exist elsewhere in Europe and beyond, in both pagan and Christian contexts. The maypole, a central feature of May Day and Beltane celebrations, is believed to be a remnant of the earliest Germanic

tribal rituals, which would have focused on a living tree, as opposed to a cut pole. And the Christmas tree, of course, is an adaptation of the Yule celebrations of old. It is believed that Christian missionaries in the Early Middle Ages essentially coopted the native beliefs and rituals of the local people by bringing their traditional object of worship—the evergreen tree—into the celebration of the newly imposed holiday instead. Despite the church's best efforts, however, trees have remained mystical, magical, and sacred to many modern-day descendants of the ancient Germans.

TREES IN WICCAN COSMOLOGY

WHEN COMPARED TO THE RELIGIOUS TRADITIONS OF THE Celts and the ancient Germans, the central tenets and practices of traditional Wicca are not quite as heavily focused on trees. The origins of what we now call Wicca, as developed by Gerald Gardner and others in the mid-twentieth century, seem to have largely emphasized worship of the Goddess and God, the celebration of fertility, and the natural cycles of life and death. And in terms of ritual practice, Gardner was more influenced by medieval occult texts and ceremonial magic than by the remnants of Druidic or Germanic lore and customs. That being said, Gardner's first real experiences with what he referred to as Witchcraft took place in the area of England known as New Forest, which was also the name of the coven he is said to have been initiated into, and he named his own coven Bricket Wood, after the village of the same name in Hertfordshire County where the coven would meet. Both of these were already names of places, of course, but they nonetheless carried an acknowledgment of the sacred quality of the forest.

When it comes to Wiccan cosmology, trees are obviously a part of Nature, and therefore they are part of the realm of the Goddess and the God. One of the chief archetypes in Wiccan deity is the God of the Forest, also known as the God of the Hunt, so trees certainly have a place of importance in the traditional Wiccan worldview. Additional archetypes worshipped in some Wiccan traditions include the Oak King and the Holly King, and the Green Man (or Green Woman). Furthermore, trees are intricately connected with the Wheel of the Year and can be seen as excellent representatives of the Elements. Next, we'll take a closer look at these important components of modern Wicca.

The Oak King and the Holly King

One way in which trees show up in some Wiccan traditions specifically is in the legend of the Oak King and the Holly King. Said to be Celtic in origin, the tale presents the Oak King as the ruler of summer and the light half of the year, while the Holly King rules winter and the dark half. The eternal turning of the two halves of the year is represented by a battle between the two kings, who are seen as rival brothers, each fighting for dominance and taking turns conquering the other. In some versions of the legend, the winning king actually kills the other, but each is always reborn, to rise and grow in strength until he reigns again.

The oak and holly trees were particularly significant to the Druids, who met for rituals in oak groves and used holly for decorating at the Winter Solstice. Their somewhat similar-looking leaves, their coexistence in northern forests, and their considerable differences make them rather appropriate for a legend about sibling rivals who take turns reigning over the world. In the summer months, oak trees make a mighty impression with their height and far-reaching branches thick with elegantly shaped

leaves. Holly, by contrast, is generally quite short and blends in with the greenery of all the other low-growing trees. Once all the deciduous trees have dropped their leaves, however, the bright, shining leaves of the holly remain to get all the attention, and the red berries they produce in the cold season provide extra cheer.

Introduced into modern paganism by Robert Graves via *The White Goddess* and later incorporated into Wiccan practice by Britons Janet and Stewart Farrar, the Oak King and Holly King have been adapted by some as aspects of the God, in addition to his more traditional aspects of the Sun and the Horned God of the forest. However, for many others, the tale is seen simply as a metaphor for the sometimes-fierce back-and-forth dance between the seasons as the Wheel of the Year continues to turn.

The battles between the two kings are often reenacted in group rituals at the appropriate Sabbats. In some versions of the legend, the Oak King wins the battle at the Spring Equinox, or Ostara, when the balance of light and dark officially tips toward the Summer Solstice. The Holly King then takes over at the Autumnal Equinox, or Mabon, when the balance tips back toward winter. In other traditions, the battles and resulting change in power occur at the solstices themselves—Litha and Yule. But no matter which calendar is followed, this story of the ongoing tug-of-war between the two brothers is often used to illustrate the nature of duality—light cannot exist without the dark, just as life cannot exist without death.

In centuries past, before the benefit of artificial lighting, the difference between the "dark" and "light" halves of the year would certainly have been more stark than what we experience today, with much more in the way of real-life consequences for the people. Viewed this way, it makes sense that the turning of the seasons might be viewed in the harsh terms of battle, victory, and death—especially in cultures accustomed to constant skirmishes and wars. In the twenty-first century, however, some contemporary Wiccans aren't crazy about the "fight" aspect of the legend, pointing out that in their native habitat, the trees are no threat to each other, and that in any case the prevailing cosmology of Wicca isn't about conflict or competition, but rather cooperation and harmony between all aspects of Nature. So some choose to observe the Oak King and Holly King as mere representatives of the seasons, each stepping forth into the spotlight and back again according to their nature. Others leave the legend out of their practice altogether.

The Green Man (and Green Woman)

Another tree-related archetype that some Wiccans incorporate into their practice is the Green Man. Arguably older and much more widespread than the legend of the Oak King and Holly King, the Green Man is an ancient symbol that has been carved into churches, cathedrals, and other public buildings since at least the days of ancient Rome, but the image is theorized to be even older. There are many variations of the symbol, but typically the Green Man is presented as a face either composed of or surrounded by leaves and vines, as if he is hiding in the forest and just barely visible. In some versions, he has vines or branches coming out of his mouth, ears, nose, or eyes as well. In several cases he has a body as well as a head, though the face alone is what we typically think of when it comes to the Green Man.

He is often cited as being a Celtic symbol and has been connected specifically with the god Cernunnos. But while he is found throughout Celtic Europe (though predominantly in Britain and France), he also appears in parts of India and the Middle East. So it would seem that our Western version of this archetype may have grown out of something older and more universal. Yet the Green Man got his English name only in the early to mid-twentieth century, when British folklorist Lady Raglan connected these symbols on English churches to the Jack o' the Green, a mythical figure in English folk traditions. This figure symbolized the fertility and new growth of the spring season, and was often part of May Day (Beltane) celebrations, represented by a man wearing a very tall costume made of leaves.

While most of the Green Man carvings around the world do seem to depict a male face, many observers have noted the presence of a Green Woman in more than a few instances. In some images, the Green Woman is giving birth to the leaves and vines, and as such has been connected to the Sheela-na-gig, a naked female figure believed to symbolize both fertility and protection from the evil eye. (The classic Sheela-na-gig image is found most often in Ireland and does not typically include tree imagery. Nonetheless, a few exceptions do exist, tying these two mysterious archetypes together.)

Many hold that the Green Man (or Green Woman) represents the spiritual presence one often feels when walking through a forest. It's as if some unseen sentient being is watching as we make our way along a path or stop to observe the sounds of birds and other animals. As the trees begin to leaf out in the spring, becoming fully lush during the summer, they hide much from view, filling in the empty spaces that had been left by the winter months of bare branches. In this sense, the Green Man can be said to represent the divinity hidden in plain sight that such greenery often evokes.

In some traditions of Wicca, the Green Man is seen as an aspect of the God, in addition to his aspects of the Sun God and the Horned God of the forest. This aspect is celebrated specifically during the warm-weather Sabbats, starting with Beltane in May and in some cases going all the way through to Mabon, the Autumnal Equinox. There is not an exact female equivalent in the sense of the Green Woman as an aspect of the Goddess, but a parallel can be drawn nonetheless to the Mother Earth aspect of the female deity. At any rate, whether we consider the male or female version of the figure or both, the imagery is a fitting one to associate with Wicca and Witchcraft at large.

The Wheel and the Elements

Aside from these somewhat eclectic archetypes (or, for some, aspects of deity), there is much about trees themselves that make them emblematic of the spirit and natural focus of Wicca. Deciduous trees, for starters, are especially perfect embodiments of the cycles of the seasons in their own right, serving as pivotal markers on the Wheel of the Year. Trees provide us with some of the first signs of spring, as subtle, velvety buds begin to emerge at the tips of otherwise bare branches. As the weather warms, the buds begin to open as blossoms and the tiniest starts of the leaves push through into the light. Leaves continue to grow as the days lengthen, with most trees in full leaf by early summer. Like the agricultural societies who gave us much of our pagan lore and tradition, the trees themselves are busy all summer long, capturing the energy of the Sun and converting it into the food they need to continue living through the dark winter months.

As the daylight wanes and autumn grows nearer, some of the first leaves will begin to turn and fall from the trees. Like our ancestors, they are preparing for winter now in earnest, producing fruits to ensure the future survival of their species, as well as the buds that their new leaves will grow from when the strong Sun returns. Soon, all the leaves will fall from their perches, but not before blazing with the colors of the Sun as a final salute before the annual "death" of the light. Once all the branches are bare and stark against graying skies, we know that the dormant winter season is upon us. It will be a few long months before the trees signal to us again that the light and warmth are making their return.

Trees, like other plant life, are also ultimate embodiments of the Elements in action. In addition to being homes for nymphs, faeries, and other Elemental beings, they represent each of the Elemental forces in unique ways. Trees are solid and literally rooted in the soil. They require at least some amount of water to survive. Trees that grow along the banks of creeks and rivers help to prevent floods, as the roots aid in preventing soil erosion. In this way trees participate in the relationship between the Element of Water and the Element of Earth.

Trees work with the air in the form of wind: breezes carry tree seeds to new locations, ensuring the reproduction of their species. Their swaying branches can also warn us of coming winds and storms.

Trees co-create with the Element of Fire, because their growth is spurred by sunlight and they literally transform the energy of light into nutritional substance. And the destructive force of fire clears out overgrown forest-floor cover that can choke out new life in order to allow the forest as a whole to continue to thrive.

Of course, like everything else on the Earth plane, trees are suffused with the Fifth Element—Spirit, or Akasha, the unifying Element that is present in every particle of the Universe. But there is also just something about a grove of trees—a sense of mystery, of "otherworldliness," a distinct energy that commands our attention and reverence. Whether we understand this energy as the presence of individual spirits, faeries, or aspects of deity, or even something less defined, there's no denying that trees truly embody the Element of Spirit.

Clearly, trees are inextricably interconnected with all of Nature, and therefore so is tree magic. We can see this easily through the lens of the Elements and the energies that each can lend to our magic when called upon. Tree magic can be worked with the Element of Air simply by watching leaves flutter in the wind and observing images and messages that come through in their dance. The Element of Earth can be honored in the ritual planting of new trees and in any spells that involve burying a charm made from bark, leaves, nuts, fruits, or blossoms. Spells and rituals that call for setting energy-infused leaves or bark to float on streams, rivers, lakes, or oceans are drawing on the Element of Water. And the Element of Fire, of course, is present for every ritual fire and any candle spell incorporating tree ingredients.

Trees and Tools of the Craft

In addition to the roles trees play in Wiccan beliefs and philosophies, they also provide the raw materials for important components of Craft practice. Many an old tree stump has been used as an altar for outdoor rituals, and groves are still a beloved place to worship the God and Goddess. When it comes to ritual tools, there are three powerful tree-based treasures still in use today that can be traced back through our ancestral lineage for millennia: the wand (or stave), the broom (or besom), and the bonfire (or balefire).

The Wand

In Wicca and many other forms modern paganism, the wand is a sacred tool. Depending on the tradition one follows (or one's individual eclectic practice), the wand may be used in ritual, spellwork (especially in ceremonial magic), meditation, and/or astral journeying. The wand has a long history, going back at least as far as the Zoroastrian religion of the sixth century BCE, when priests used a barsom—a bundle of twigs—to establish a link between the material and spiritual realms. A similar bundle was used by the ancient priests (flamines) of Rome. As we saw earlier, the Druids of the ancient Celts and the Norse seeresses also used wands for magic. Wands also appear in ancient Greek myth, as well as in records of magic spells from Egypt. These ancient societies in turn influenced the practices of medieval magicians, who included much lore and instruction regarding wands in their magical texts, known as grimoires.

But the wand is not just a tool of European origin. Shamanic traditions from Africa to Asia to South America have employed wands in a variety of ways. Actually, the wand is only one type of a broader category of magical tools made from trees, known as staves. A stave can be a wand, a staff, a stang (a forked staff), or other rod-shaped tool. The staff, a much longer and quite possibly much older version of the wand, has been a symbol of power and leadership in many different religions around the world, including Christianity. It is held during rituals and carried during travel by shamans, magicians, and healers alike. Among our pagan ancestors, the staff was used for protective magic, directing energy, and invoking spiritual entities, among other things.

Like the wand, the staff is mentioned often in medieval grimoires, and the two tools are considered to have the same magical powers and uses. The chief difference between them is size—a staff is typically long enough to be used as a walking stick, while a wand is usually no longer than a foot or so and is often tapered at one end. While the staff is less prevalent than the wand in Wiccan practice, it is incorporated into some forms of Wicca and many other traditions within the wider world of modern Witchcraft. For the sake of simplicity, this guide will focus only on the wand, but if you would like to work with a staff instead or with both, then by all means do so!

With some notable exceptions, such as the bronze staffs of the Norse *völur* mentioned earlier, and the metal and ivory wands of the ancient Egyptians, the wands of our pagan ancestors were typically made from the branches of trees. This choice was not simply down to whether other materials were available—in fact, wood was still the preferred option for many practitioners. For while we know that metal is a conductor of electricity, wood is actually a means through which other kinds of energy can be transmitted. We've already seen that trees were considered by the ancients to be a link between the physical and spiritual realms. It follows then that the branches of trees could serve this function as well, in a manner that allows the wand's user to specifically direct the energy of this connection.

In some traditions, particularly those inspired by the ancient Celts, it is the spirit of the tree the wand is made from that facilitates the magical action being performed. The wand becomes an extension of the spiritual energy of the individual tree, as well as the archetypal spirit of the species of tree it was made from. Therefore, a wand made from an oak branch will have different energetic properties than a wand made from the branch of a hazel or rowan tree. However, as with any magical tool, a wand in and of itself has no real power. It is the joining of the will, or intent, of the magician with the energetic capacities of the wand that makes magic happen. Some say that the wand is a representation of the magician's will, which is ultimately true, but the same can be said of other magical tools and spell ingredients. It may be more accurate in this case to say that the wand is used to focus and direct the energy of the intention, or will, of its user. Its linear shape enables a clear visualization of both the energy itself and the des-

tination to which it is sent. It can almost be compared to a pointer used by a presenter in a lecture hall, only the lecturer is you, and the audience is the spiritual entities you are working with, whether they be Elemental beings, specific deities, or simply the energies of the Universe in general.

Wands are used for a variety of purposes in Wiccan and other contemporary pagan ritual and magic. On the altar, the wand can be used to represent the God, as well as the Element of

Fire or Air, depending on the tradition. The wand and athame, or ritual knife, serve similar functions and may be used interchangeably for certain aspects of ritual. In ceremonial-inspired magic, the wand is used to tap or point to specific components (or ingredients) of a spell, infusing them with magical energy, and to draw runes and other magical symbols in the air over the work. They can also be used to send the cumulative energy of the spell in a specific direction, known in some circles as "blasting."

Wands have also been used to invoke spirits as well as to send them back to where they came from. In their traditional shamanic capacity, wands can serve to open the "doors" between the material and spiritual realms, facilitating safe astral travel. Wands have also been used as divining tools, or dowsers, helping to find underground sources of water and other secrets hidden under the Earth, such as ancient burial sites.

The art of wand making is a tradition in and of itself, and the old grimoires are full of various instructions and specifications for doing so. *The Key of Solomon*, for example, recommends elder and hazel as ideal wand wood, and Wednesday at sunrise as the best time for harvesting the branch. Various sources recommend different lengths, widths, and materials, as well as rituals for consecrating the newly made wand. It is ideal, ultimately, to make your own wand, because then it is infused from the beginning with your own unique personal energy. But of course, this isn't strictly necessary, and if you feel drawn to purchase a wand made by another, then that is the best wand for you at this point on your personal path. If you do want to make your own tree-sourced wand, however, you'll find some suggestions for doing so in part 3 of this guide.

The Broom

The broom, of course, remains a hallmark image of the stereo-typical fantasy "witch" in mainstream culture, serving as a lit-eral vehicle for those with the magical know-how to soar into the night sky. Actual Witches know that flying is symbolic of astral travel, which can be achieved with (or without) the assistance of certain psychotropic plants. Recipes for "flying ointments" are found in sources dating back to ancient times. (However, many of

these contained toxic ingredients, and it is not recommended to try them yourself!) The origins of the association between broom-sticks and flying may be related to the use of flying ointments, but a more likely source is an old pagan fertility ritual that involved "riding" astride broomsticks, pitchforks, and other pole-shaped objects through agricultural fields while jumping high into the air, to encourage crops to grow.

At any rate, many long-standing pagan traditions have incor-porated the humble broom. In handfasting customs in Wales, the newlyweds would jump over a broomstick together for fertility. The Celts were said to associate the broom with the faerie realm. Some legends told of Witches who sought the faeries' assistance in finding the perfect branch in the forest for making a magical broom.

Brooms were used to clear out negative energy from the home and to prepare a household energetically for the birth of a child. They were also placed upright near the door of the home, or hung horizontally above the door, for protection. Traditionally, a broom for use in magic, known as a besom, was made with a handle of hazel, ash, or oak, and bristles made from birch twigs. Thin strips of willow wood held the bristles to the handle. It is said that a few ancient besoms have been found with secret compartments inside the handle that held herbs, oils, and other potential spell ingredients. Whether or not this is the case, it's easy to see how a seemingly common household implement could help Witches disguise their Craft during the perilous witch hunts of the Middle Ages.

Today, sacred brooms are still placed against or near doors to protect the home from unwanted visitors (both from the Earth plane and from the spiritual realm). They are also used to ritually sweep out stale or negative energy from indoor environments and to prepare sacred space before ritual. (Typically, the bristles of a sacred broom never touch the floor—the "sweeping" is more symbolic, but still serves its energetic purpose.) Some Wiccans use a besom to close the circle at the end of ritual, dispersing any leftover energies, but beyond these purposes it is not typically considered a core ritual tool. In many Craft traditions, the broom is associated with the Element of Water, due to its purifying function, and is sacred to the Goddess. However, other traditions view the broom as evenly balanced between the genders, with the handle representing the divine masculine, and the bristles the divine feminine.

Like the wand, the broom can be made from wood chosen for its particular magical energies. But unlike the wand, the broom also has a mundane purpose and therefore can be a magical tool hidden in plain sight within the home, which works well for Witches who aren't "out of the broom closet" and practice in complete secrecy. Whether it's a common household broom or the small, decorative kind, your "besom in disguise" can still be used to guard your door, and no one will be the wiser. A regular household broom can be a handy alternative to harvesting twigs and branches to make your own or buying a special besom in a magical supply shop. You can simply charge a normal broom—preferably one with a wooden handle—to use for ritual purposes. Just make sure it's a brand-new broom and that you don't use it for regular household cleaning. Or, if you prefer, you can just use a tree branch—preferably one with smaller, twig-sized branches still attached—as a symbolic broom for the ritual sweeping of a space.

The Bonfire

There can be no fire without fuel, and trees have provided fuel for the fires that have kept us warm and nourished since humans first discovered it. Many Wiccan and other pagan traditions celebrate the Sabbats with a ritual bonfire, especially during Beltane, Litha, and Samhain. These fires are known as balefires in Celtic-influenced traditions, a term stemming from the ancient fire festival of Beltane in early Ireland. Falling at the beginning of May, the traditional start to summer in the Celtic world, Beltane honored the ancient Sun god Bel. The smoke from the sacred Beltane fires was used to purify the community's cattle and crops for the season, and embers from the central "Bel-fire" (or Bealtaine, in Irish Gaelic) were used to relight hearth fires throughout the land. Of course, many other ancient European pagan cultures held ritual and celebratory fires as well, including the Greeks, Romans, and Norse.

Many forms of Wicca observe a tradition of "nine sacred woods," a list of nine different types of trees whose wood is considered the most magical for burning in a ritual fire. Special fires, such as those at Beltane, might be composed of all nine, though since this is often not practical, a combination of two or more may be used. Like the balefire itself, this tradition also traces back to Celtic lore, where several references to nine sacred (or "blessed") trees can be found among mythology, poetry, and song. The types of trees vary from source to source, but most include oak, rowan, willow, hawthorn, and hazel. Other trees named in some sources but not others include ash, holly, apple, elm, and alder. Ultimately, the differences among the Celtic references might simply have depended upon location, as it would be most practical to use whatever wood could be found near one's home.

The modern poem known as "The Wiccan Rede" includes a mention of "nine woods," which are usually interpreted as birch, oak, rowan, willow, hawthorn, hazel, apple, fir, and elder. These nine are viewed by some Wiccans as the appropriate "sacred woods" for ritual fires. However, it's unclear whether this part of the "Rede" is a direct reference to the ancient tradition of the bale-fire, since it's the "cauldron" into which the woods are said to go, and the next line of this passage warns against burning elder, lest one be cursed. (Elder is strongly associated with Witches and death in medieval lore, and also makes very poor firewood, which may explain this particular warning.) Another potential source for selecting the appropriate nine trees is the Celtic tree calendar described on page 16. The first nine trees of the calendar are birch, rowan, ash, alder, willow, hawthorn, oak, holly, and hazel.

Along with the special Sabbat fires, covens as well as solitary Witches may honor the Full Moon with a ritual bonfire, choosing wood that fits the ritual theme or magical goal(s) of the gathering.

If you're fortunate enough to have a working fireplace in your home, you can also integrate this practice into your magic by burning purpose-appropriate wood in the hearth during rituals and spellwork. For example, you might burn oak in the fireplace while working spells for healing or prosperity, and apple or maple for love magic.

If you choose to incorporate ritual fire into your practice, be sure to acquire your firewood in the most ecologically responsible way possible. When purchasing, look for wood from certified-sustainable sources so you're not supporting reckless deforestation. If you're out foraging for your bonfire, leave hollow logs alone, as they provide homes for woodland animals. Whenever possible, source your firewood from fallen trees and consider using recycled wood fuel in lieu of virgin wood in your home hearth. These are good ways to respect the spiritual energies of the tree kingdom and the Earth as a whole, while still enjoying an age-old magical tradition.

THE MAGICAL ENERGY OF FLOWERS

WHILE THEY MAY BE MUCH SMALLER AND MORE FRAGILE than our mighty tree friends, flowers are every bit as fascinating and magical. If you've ever spent time closely observing a flower in detail, you'll probably have noticed its structural complexity and quick responsiveness to changing environmental conditions such as light, wind, and moisture. Simply observing flowers as they unfold over the course of a day is an enchanting experience. If you've never seen a time-lapse video of flowers blooming, it's worth finding one to witness their magic at work.

Flowers also have extremely brief lifespans in comparison to trees. While many flowering plants are perennial and bloom each year, the flowers themselves still die and disintegrate after a little while. This means that flower magic often requires more precise timing than spellwork involving trees, as the flower itself will not exist for long. Working with local wildflowers, for example, involves an awareness of their particular seasons. Spells that call for these flowers may be worked only at the time of year when they're in bloom or must utilize dried petals gathered during the blooming season.

Flower magic is really a branch of herbal magic, as all flowering plants are technically herbs. But the focus here, of course, is on the flower of the plant, as opposed to its leaves, roots, or seeds. The flower itself is an expression of the whole plant's energy. And since flowering plants aren't always in bloom, the flower contains the specific energy available at that time in the plant's life cycle.

Each type of flower has its own unique energy, which can be drawn on for magical work.

Flower Folk Magic

The availability of cut flowers from just about anywhere in the world today has given rise to new forms of flower magic that wouldn't have been practical in the days of our pagan ancestors. We can buy flowers from a store or a farmers' market, as opposed to having to grow or forage for them in the wild, and we don't have to wait until they're in season in our area. This expanded availability grants us access to a much wider variety of flowers than any time before.

In contrast, our ancestors would have had a more holistic relationship with the whole plant—not just the blooms themselves, but the foliage, roots, seeds, and soil needed to produce the flowers in the first place. They were working with what grew around them, or cultivating the seeds they had access to—which would still largely have been native to the area, rather than imported from halfway around the world. They noted the overall ecosystem that the flowering plants were part of, rather than seeing the flowers as separate, unrelated objects. For example, as we saw earlier, mistletoe was significant to the Druids not just for its white flowers, but because of its ecological relationship with the oak tree.

The relationship between flowers and the turning of the seasons would also have been noted by the ancients. Various perennial wildflowers bloom at different points in the spring, summer, and even early autumn in some areas. Even today, the appearance of the first dandelions tells us that spring has arrived, and keen observers of wildflowers can predict the coming weather based on the appearance of the blooms. Flowers were part of many seasonal festival celebrations, such as those held on May Day (or Beltane) and Midsummer (the Summer Solstice).

Tree blossoms and spring wildflowers were gathered at dawn and woven into crowns and garlands for May Day. Flowers were also used to decorate houses and the village maypole. Farmers would rub buttercup flowers on the udders of their cows on this day to increase their milk supply, as well as to protect them from faeries. (The term *faerie* is often nebulously defined and can refer to many different kinds of nature spirits from various cultures. So it's likely that the faeries feared by the ancestors are not the same beings sought out by Witches.) In some areas, the flowering plant known as St. John's wort was heralded on the Summer Solstice (also known as St. John's Day) for its ability to protect households and farms from evil spirits.

Flowers were also used in ritual and deity worship. The Druids and Romans incorporated blue vervain into their ceremonial rites. The Norse honored the goddess Freya with columbine. Violets in ancient Greece were considered sacred to the god Cupid. Foxglove, also known as witch's glove, was used in pagan rituals to break enchantments placed by the faeries. In some Slavic areas today, flower wreaths are still thrown into local bodies of water during Summer Solstice celebrations.

Of course, there were plenty of folk beliefs surrounding flowers. For example, it was believed that bringing yellow poppies into the house would cause misfortune, usually in the form of bad weather or headaches. Walking in a counterclockwise circle three times around a snapdragon was said to remove negative energy attachments or unclear thinking caused by black magic. Wearing a crown of violets was thought to help improve sleep and relieve headaches. Flowers were also used in romantic divination. The most well-known divination is probably the ritual of saying, "He loves me; he loves me not," while pulling petals off a daisy. Another involved eating five lilac petals one after another. If none of the petals stuck to the person's tongue, then the love interest's feelings were mutual.

These and other folk beliefs around flowers were the foundations of a tradition that emerged in the 1800s known as floriography, or the language of flowers. During the Victorian era, it wasn't socially acceptable to be open and honest with one's feelings toward members of the opposite sex. Flowers were used symbolically to express these feelings when given as bouquets, stitched onto pillows or clothing, or even incorporated into paintings. Each type of flower represented a specific emotion or message. Daffodils carried connotations of respect and chivalry, for example, while marigolds could be interpreted as restless passion. So bouquets given to a potential mate were not necessarily made of only the prettiest flowers available at the time. They were also coded love letters.

Today, Wiccans and other Witches incorporate flowers into their ritual and magical practices in a variety of ways. Flower wreaths are crafted for the summer Sabbats (especially Beltane and Litha), and altar decorations often include flowers, whether they're cut stems in a vase or petals scattered around the altar. Flower petals may also be used to mark the sacred circle before ritual. Flowers are used in offerings to deities and nature spirits, in ritual baths, and in many other kinds of spellwork. Witches who enjoy creating magical crafts may use flowers in incense recipes, spell sachets, and poppets and to create flower-infused magical oils. Kitchen Witches might use edible flowers in magical potions and culinary spells. And, of course, simply having flowers around the home helps keep the vibrational atmosphere higher, as these are some of Nature's most exquisite expressions of spiritual energy.

NATURE SPIRITS: ELEMENTALS AND THE GENIUS LOCI

BEING NONPHYSICAL, NATURE SPIRITS ARE OBVIOUSLY MORE difficult to define and categorize than trees, flowers, or any other physical natural phenomena. But that certainly doesn't mean they don't exist! Nonphysical entities have been perceived and described in a variety of ways in animistic cultures all over the world since the beginning of recorded history. From the Greek dryads (tree spirits) and Norse *landvaettir* (land spirits) to the Nibiinaabe (water spirits) of the North American Ojibwe and the "guardians" of Nature among the San of South Africa, these spirit-plane beings have so many names, forms, and associated myths and legends that it would take an entire book to do the topic justice.

Since Wicca can't be traced back to one single indigenous culture, there's no standardized vocabulary for nature spirits within Wiccan traditions. However, many refer to these beings as Elementals: entities that exist within the four Elements of Earth, Air, Fire, and Water. This concept grew out of the writings of alchemists and other occult scholars working within the Western Mystery Tradition during the sixteenth century, who sought to categorize the beings from older mythology and folklore according to the four classical Elements of ancient Greek philosophy. Earth Elementals are often known as faeries (or fairies), gnomes, or elves, while Fire Elementals are called salamanders. Air Elementals are usually referred to as sylphs, and Water Elementals are undines; both of these terms were coined by the sixteenth-century Swiss

alchemist Paracelsus. Many Wiccans and other Witches call on Elementals to attend their rituals, including these beings in their invocation of the Elements themselves.

Furthermore, Elementals are not necessarily considered "spirits" by everyone who works with them. For some, they're more like interdimensional beings that are invisible to most humans, with physical, often human-like attributes. They are also not necessarily only found in Nature. The brownies (or *brùnaidh*) of Scotland, for example, are said to live in households and help with chores at night when no one's looking. Again, there's really no way to neatly describe what Elementals are, given such a diverse field of belief and tradition.

Another type of nonphysical nature spirit was described by the ancient Romans as the genius loci (plural: *genii locorum*) or "spirit of a place." Known by various names across many other cultures, these protective spirits are distinct energies that reside in or around a specific place or object in Nature, such as a meadow, a tree, or an entire mountain. Like Elementals, they are typically invisible to the human eye, though some people do catch glimpses of them from time to time. However, genii locorum are not necessarily going to answer to Wiccan ritual invocations. These nature spirits are more interested in protecting their particular habitat in Nature than participating in any human ritual activity.

In fact, nature spirits are often distrustful of humans, and with good reason: We have not been taking good care of the Earth! Nonetheless, Witches with good sixth-sense perception and appropriate respect for all inhabitants of Nature, physical and nonphysical, can and do communicate with genius loci in their practice. We'll take a look at suggestions for how to approach making this connection in the section "Connecting with Nature Spirits," pages 100–102.

It's important to understand that everyone perceives and interacts differently with the energies of Nature, which is why there are so many different names and concepts for describing them. Some Witches may use a catch-all term for these beings, such as "Elementals," "faeries," or simply "nature spirits," while others recognize distinctions between faeries, gnomes, sprites, sylphs, and so on. Some people perceive Elementals as being one and the same as nature spirits. Others experience these two categories as separate energetic phenomena and may work with either one or both. Don't worry if you're uncertain about the terminology around nature spirits or whether you're perceiving these energies "correctly." Remember that everything in the Universe is ultimately part of the same whole, and each individual plant, flower, tree, animal, spirit entity, and human being is an individual expression of divine energy. When you seek to commune with Nature, what you resonate with on a personal level is what you're meant to tune in to.

GETTING UP CLOSE
AND PERSONAL

TUNING IN TO THE ENERGIES OF NATURE DOESN'T REQUIRE any specialized knowledge of botany or ecology. But the more you can learn about the individual living beings in your midst, the deeper your connection and appreciation can be. Furthermore, when you have a working knowledge of the magical energies of specific species of plant life, your spellwork becomes more powerful.

In part 2, you'll meet thirteen trees and thirteen flowers with long-standing magical reputations, and you'll discover their individual properties and uses. There are also practical suggestions for learning how to connect with nonphysical nature spirits. So get ready to get up close and personal with these magical allies, and let your magic blossom!

PART TWO
TREES, FLOWERS, AND NATURE SPIRITS

NATURE'S MAGICAL INHABITANTS

WICCANS AND OTHER WITCHES ARE TYPICALLY AMONG THE most ardent nature lovers you can find. However, that doesn't mean we're all avid hikers or well versed in tree identification or the intricacies of gardening. There are plenty of Witches who work regularly with dried herbs from magical supply shops yet wouldn't be able to recognize the plants they come from if their lives depended on it. But this shouldn't be considered a failing. In fact, one of the perks of the twenty-first century is that we have such easy access to magical ingredients from all over the world.

That said, taking your practice further by learning all you can about the living sources of these ingredients is well worth the effort. To that end, the following pages will introduce you to the history, lore, and unique characteristics of trees and flowers commonly used in magic. You'll also find tips for forming more intentional energetic connections with the energies of Nature and opening up to the magical wisdom they have to offer.

THIRTEEN MAGICAL TREES

THE TREES FEATURED ON THE FOLLOWING PAGES HAVE BEEN regarded as magical and/or sacred by cultures in both the Old World and the New World. (One exception is maple, which evidently was not considered an important magical tree in the Old World but is highly valued by the descendants of Native North Americans and immigrants alike.) Because Wicca and other forms of the Craft came to North America via Europe, the history and lore, medicinal uses, and magical uses and associations are, on the whole, derived from European rather than Native American traditions, with the exception of a few brief details.

The descriptions in this section are largely generalized to the common name for each tree, rather than individual species, which often have their own more specified magical uses and associations. You can apply the information here to any species of the tree or do some research into each individual species for even more information. For example, if you live in the desert in the American Southwest, you can work with emory oak the same way you'd work with white oak in the Midwest. But you can also look into magical aspects of emory oak that may differ from those of white oak and tweak your spellwork accordingly.

Depending on where you live, some or many of these trees may not be native to your area. In addition, be aware that the lists of example species for each tree are by no means exhaustive, so it's well worth doing your own research to see what additional species might grow in your area. Finally, you may find plenty of cultivated

trees in yards, parks, and other public areas that are not native to your area but rather imported from elsewhere. It really doesn't matter in the slightest to your magic, so work with whatever trees are near you!

Finally, a cautionary note: The medical uses described here are for informational purposes only and are not intended to serve as instructional, nor should they be used in place of needed medical care by a physician. Also, many of the medicinal uses of certain plants still require further research as to their effectiveness. If you decide to experiment with any part of any tree for healing purposes, be sure to research thoroughly and know that in this context, the particular species of plant is *very* important to identify, as not all species will have the same physiological effects on the human body; and, always consult first with your health care practitioner.

Ash

(*FRAXINUS* SPP.)

Range of native habitat: all regions of continental US, eastern and western Canada, Europe, and Asia

The ash genus consists of roughly 65 species, most of which reach between 40 and 60 feet (12–14 m) in height at maturity. Technically, the ash "leaf" is a set of individual "leaflets" that grow in pairs directly opposite each other on the stem, with a single leaflet at the end. Ash has strong, thick twigs and a large, deep root system. Some species are threatened by an invasive beetle called the emerald ash borer, which feeds on the bark of native ash. Ash is sometimes confused with mountain ash, which is a common name in North America for rowan trees, but they are not related.

Among our pagan ancestors, the ash was a highly significant tree. In origin stories from both ancient Greece and Scandinavia, the first human man was created from an ash tree. The Celts viewed the ash as the connector of the three interlinking circles of existence—past, present, and future—and it is one of the faerie triad of trees (along with oak and hawthorn). Druids made wands and magical charms from ash wood, and it has long served as the wood for the handle of the besom, or ritual broom, in traditional Witchcraft.

Ash was seen as having protective and healing properties, particularly when it came to children. In Ireland, an energy healer (or "faerie doctor") would often hold a wand of ash during ritual prayer. In Britain, a small amount of ash sap was once fed to newborn babies to keep them healthy. Ill or injured children were brought to a young ash or sapling and passed naked through a cleft cut into the tree, which was then bound together to heal as the child healed. In some places it was believed that the tree and the child were connected for life, so the tree was watched over and often studded with nails to prevent it from being cut down for its wood.

Ash was a traditional wood for the Yule log, and, as we saw in part 1 (see pages 18–19), it has long been thought to be Yggdrasil, or the World Tree, of Norse cosmology. Although it is now believed by scholars that this was not the case, the association is widespread and longstanding enough that any energetic association one feels with the ash in this context is perfectly valid. Either way, it is still known as a tree of enchantment, of timelessness, of existing between and across the visible and invisible worlds.

Ash bark is thought by some healers to have astringent and diuretic properties, and has been used in infusions to treat liver and intestinal issues, rheumatism, and malaria. It was also used to reduce fevers and soothe sore throats, and to relieve kidney and urinary infections. A tea made from the leaves of European ash was used to treat jaundice, rheumatism, and gout. Ash can interact with some medications, such as those for diabetes and high blood pressure, so consult your physician first. Ash tree and flower essences aid with self-knowledge and trusting in one's own authority.

Magically, ash is used for protection (especially during travel on or near water), prosperity, healing, wisdom, and spiritual growth. Ash connects us to the unseen realms and the liminal spaces outside linear time, and so is particularly good for prophetic dreaming. Place fresh ash leaves under your pillow for clearer and more enhanced dreams, and be sure to write down anything of significance the next morning. As the connecting point between past, present, and future, it puts us in touch with the energy of creation, making it an excellent ally in workings related to creativity (especially the literary arts).

To promote good health, place a few fresh ash leaves in a bowl of blessed water near your bed before going to sleep. The bark can also be added to witch jars and poppets for protection. For prosperity, burn a log of ash at Yule, or use ash bark as loose incense. Make charms for healing, love, or prosperity out of small ash twigs and carry them with you until your desire has manifested.

Ash wood is a good conductor of energy and makes excellent wands, particularly for the purpose of astral travel and healing, but also for workings related to personal transformation, balance, harmony, and rain magic.

✦ MAGICAL ASSOCIATIONS ✦

GENDER: Masculine, Feminine

ELEMENT: Fire, Air, Water

PLANET: Sun, Neptune

ZODIAC: Pisces, Aries

DEITIES: Poseidon, Jupiter, Mars, Minerva, Odin, Thor, Frigg, Lir, Manannán

Birch

(*BETULA* SPP.)

Range of native habitat: Throughout cooler regions of the Northern Hemisphere

A slender yet deceptively hardy tree, birch is most often associated with the bright white bark of the paper birch species, although there are approximately forty species in the *Betula* genus. In fact, the etymology of *birch* can be traced back to Indo-European words related to brilliance, brightness, shimmer, and glitter in various contemporary languages. Birches have double-toothed, slightly heart-shaped leaves and can grow to heights of 50 to 70 feet (15–21 m). One of the first trees to flower in the spring, birch is also one of the first to naturally establish after a forest has been cleared, and it was one of the first to emerge after the last ice age. Hence, birch has long been seen as a symbol of new beginnings.

In ancient Northern Europe, birch was widely seen as a protective tree, especially of women and children. Twigs and branches were brought into the home for protection, and cradles were made from the wood to keep malevolent faeries away from the child. Carrying a piece of birch was thought to protect against kidnapping by the faeries. In Scandinavia, birch trees were planted in front of the home to protect all within the household. In Ireland, people carried amulets of birch branches marked with Ogham inscriptions.

For the Celts, birch was also a tree of purification, used to drive out the "spirits of the old year" from the home, and the traditional besom, or ritual broom, was made of birch twigs. Fertility, love, and marriage were widely associated with birch. Birch twigs were used to light the Beltane fires and could be used to grant fertility to a barren cow. In the Gaulish region of Europe, birch twigs were lit during marriage ceremonies for fertility and luck. In Wales, birch branches were woven into wreaths and given as love tokens. Birch was sometimes used as the maypole tree for May Day celebrations, and couples in Scandinavia would frolic in birch to celebrate the beginning of summer. The Norse rune Berkanan translates to *birch tree* or *birch goddess* and symbolizes matters related to birth and motherhood.

Birch bark has been used by healers for treating muscle soreness, burns, wounds, and other skin conditions such as eczema. Birch bark essential oil has also been used as an insect repellent. The leaves have been used in a tea that was believed to treat rheumatism and gout, dissolve kidney stones, and to heal sores in the mouth. A yellow fungus known as chaga mushrooms that grows on the trunks of birches has long been used by native peoples in Russia, Poland, and other Baltic countries as a folk remedy to treat tumors. It is now gaining recognition as a possible tool in the treatment and prevention of cancer (although chaga is becoming endangered due to overharvesting).

Magically, birch is a symbol of birth, renewal, purification, and fresh starts. It is highly powerful when used in magic worked at the New Moon, for beginning new projects, for channeling divine feminine energy, and for love, beauty, and protection. Carry birch twigs or bark in a protection charm, particularly against negative energy or psychic attack. Use a besom made with birch to purify the energy of your home at the New Year, right after either Samhain or Yule, depending on your tradition.

Birch is also known as a tree of illumination, because of how well birch bark can be seen at night in a forest, especially in moonlight. This makes birch ideal for shadow work, when you need to see aspects of your inner self that are blocked and therefore holding you back from making progress in an area of your life. The tree essence is used to "peel" away old layers of self in order to allow your true self to shine through. It is also excellent for workings related to renewing energy after illness or other difficult circumstances. To release energies from a past situation, write a word or phrase representing the issue on a piece of birch bark and set it afloat on a river or stream.

GENDER: Feminine

ELEMENT: Air, Water, Fire

PLANET: Venus

ZODIAC: Sagittarius

DEITIES: Venus, Thor, Freya, Cerridwen, Brigid, Lugh, Angus Mac Og, the Dagda

Cedar

(*CEDRUS* SPP., *JUNIPERUS* SPP., *THUJA* SPP.)

Range of native habitat: *Cedrus* spp.—Western Himalayas and the Mediterranean region; *Juniperus* spp.—throughout the Northern Hemisphere and mountainous Central America; *Thuja* spp.—North America and eastern Asia

The aromatic evergreens known as cedar can be confusing to discuss, since most trees called cedar in North America are not true cedars (genus *Cedrus*), but are actually other conifers belonging to either the genus *Juniperus* or the genus *Thuja*. In fact, none of the four *Cedrus* species are native to North America. (However, the atlas cedar (*Cedrus atlantica*) was introduced into the United States in the mid-nineteenth century and has been cultivated as an ornamental tree ever since.) The trees in North America known as cedar have traits in common with the true cedars (such as appearance and aromatic wood), and so were misnamed by early pioneers in regions where these trees grow.

All three of these tree genera (*Cedrus*, *Juniperus*, and *Thuja*) are related in that they belong to the order Pinales, which includes all conifers. In this guide, true cedar is considered synonymous with the others, since we now have a history of understanding these various trees as cedar and thus have collectively manifested a sameness between them. This bears out in the similarities between magical purposes and associations for all of these trees. However, you can find more magical uses by researching each of these species on its own.

Like many conifers, cedar represents renewal and eternal life. Cedar is one of the first trees to return to areas that have been burned or cleared of vegetation, and it is used medicinally by some Native American women to restore strength after giving birth. The smoke of burning cedar has been used by native North Americans for millennia in sacred ceremonies and to repel malevolent spirits.

Cedar's preservative properties were employed by the ancient Celts on the severed heads of their defeated enemies (the head being seen as the "seat of the soul" in Celtic culture), and by Egyptians in the embalming process.

In aromatherapy, cedar oil helps to lift sadness and banish stress, returning one's ability to access a spiritual outlook. Communing physically with cedar trees, whether by using the essential oil, carrying a sprig in your pocket, or sitting against the trunk of a cedar, is an excellent way to rejuvenate your personal energy, particularly after experiencing hardship or expending great effort on an endeavor.

Cedar's magical properties include purification, protection, and positive energy, as well as communing with divine wisdom. It is used in charms for longevity, protection, luck, and prosperity. Cedar wands and smudge sticks are used to cleanse negative energy from homes and sacred spaces. Red cedar is particularly known for assisting with divination and finding clarity in confusing situations, as well as improving communication in general. Magical workings related to psychic protection, banishing nightmares, connecting with helpful spirits, regaining and retaining good health, and creating sacred space can all benefit from incorporating cedar.

✦ MAGICAL ASSOCIATIONS ✦

GENDER: Masculine
ELEMENT: Fire, Earth, Air
PLANET: Sun, Jupiter, Mars, Mercury
ZODIAC: Leo, Gemini, Virgo
DEITIES: Ra, Artemis, Persephone, Jupiter

Elm

(*ULMUS* SPP.)

Range of native habitat: Northern Hemisphere, Middle East, East Asia, Southeast Asia

The graceful elm can grow to be up to 150 feet (46 m) tall and has dark green leaves 4 to 6 inches (10–15 cm) in length. There are approximately 40 species of elm. Its upward-reaching branches often create a canopy that resembles a vase or an inverted triangle. Unfortunately, elms are highly susceptible to a fungus spread by the elm bark beetle. Known as Dutch elm disease, this fungus has caused the elm to become an endangered tree. However, elms can still be found throughout their native range, and those in areas unaffected by Dutch elm disease can live for several hundred years.

Many trees are associated with faeries and other nature spirits, but elm has a particular association with the elves (or *álfar* in Old Norse), a mysterious race of invisible beings that dwell in various landscapes throughout Germanic mythology. The Anglo-Saxons referred to the elm as elven, and this tree is still considered one to visit if you'd like to make contact with the wood elves. (Legends tell us this can be accomplished by sitting under an elm at night and singing until dawn.) In both Greek and Celtic myth, the elm appears in relation to the Underworld; in the British Isles it has been one of the most frequently used trees in making coffins. Elm also has an interesting association with Witches. It is said that in Britain, the species known as "wych elm" (*Ulmus glabra*) was named so because Witches met under this tree—although the etymology of the word *wych* is from the Old English *wice*, thought to be from a Germanic root meaning "bend," connoting the elm's pliable branches.

One species of elm popular in herbal medicine from past to present is slippery elm, from the North Amercian *Ulmus rubra*. The inner bark of this tree is used to treat minor colds, coughs, and sore throats. It is drunk as a tea to help speed the healing of broken bones. Slippery elm tea is believed to help nausea and menstrual issues. In tree essence form, English elm (*Ulmus minor* 'Atinia') helps calm and rejuvenate the mind, and sharpens the sixth sense. Avoid elm if pregnant or breast-feeding.

Elm is used for a variety of magical purposes, including love, protection, stability, connection with nature spirits, and connecting with the divine feminine. To attract love, make a charm using elm wood and/or flowers and wear it around your neck. You can also use ground elm in a love incense blend, or place two small elm branches on your altar for any love-related workings. For protection, powdered slippery elm bark can be sprinkled in the corners of each room or carried in a sachet in your pocket. Traditionally, elm protects against malicious gossip, and sticks of it can be tied together with a yellow cord and burned for this purpose. Use elm in workings related to fertility or rebirth, and in rituals honoring the Goddess, especially in her Crone aspect. To add stability or focus to any spell, ground yourself after ritual and magic, or gain assistance when navigating any kind of difficult transition, call on the comforting energy of this gentle tree.

GENDER: Feminine

ELEMENT: Air, Water, Earth

PLANET: Mercury, Saturn

ZODIAC: Capricorn, Pisces

DEITIES: Orpheus, Dionysus, Hecate, Gaia, Odin, Loki, Cerridwen, Danu, the Crone

Fir

(*ABIES* SPP.)

Range of native habitat: Mostly mountainous regions of North and Central America, Europe, Asia, and North Africa

The fir is a part of the larger pine family (Pinaceae) but is distinguishable from pine in that its needles are typically short (just 1 to 1.5 inches [2.5–3.8 cm]) and grow in pairs opposite each other on the stem, rather than in bundles. Their cones usually grow in upright cylinders. Some of the approximately fifty species of fir have prickly needles, while others do not—so be careful when approaching a fir for the first time!

One of many coniferous evergreens associated with immortality and the continuity of life, the fir tree was sacred to ancient deities like Artemis, a Greek goddess of childbirth, and Osiris, the Egyptian god who was killed by his jealous brother Set and then resurrected by his wife, Isis. Interestingly, the fir is also a popular choice for celebrating the Christmas holiday—the birth point of yet another birth-death-resurrection cycle. The Christmas tree tradition actually stems from ancient pagan Europe, where evergreen trees were part of midwinter ceremonies from as far south as Greece to the northern reaches of Norse and Germanic lands (see page 22).

The fir tree was also highly valued by the Druids and by various Native American tribes, who view it as a protective tree. Some use fir branches for flooring in sacred sweat lodges. Balsam fir trees have also been used in "weather sticks," branches that indicate humidity levels, which can be used to predict rain. It is said that the silver fir has a similar use, but it's the cones that indicate wet or dry weather approaching.

The resin and essential oils from the buds of fir have been used by healers to treat coughs and other respiratory issues, as well as rheumatism and gout, and to seal wounds. Fir needles can be steeped in a tea to provide extra vitamin C when fighting colds, or in the bath for soothing symptoms of rheumatism. The inner bark of some fir species is also effective for treating mild chest congestion and fevers. Some fir species are poisonous to animals, and the essential oil can be irritating to the skin, so approach medicinal use of fir with caution.

Fir's magical properties make it excellent for use in workings relating to childbirth, healing, energizing the body, and regeneration. Its needles are burned to mitigate labor pains and in ceremonies to bless mother and baby after childbirth. They can also be burned to lift negative energy from a space in order to lighten one's mood, and the tree essence aids with creativity and feelings of empowerment. Fir's association with regeneration and with insight makes it a good Dark Moon tree—commune with a fir as you seek clarity on what needs to be released in your life in order to make room for new blessings. It is also used in spellwork for youth and vitality, and bringing about or adjusting to change.

Fir is also used in prosperity magic. Place needles or cones in charms to carry in your pocket or purse for this purpose. If possible, work a prosperity spell in the presence of a fir tree, or bring its branches to your indoor altar. It can be added to charms for protection and increasing personal power, and in spells related to healing karmic issues. Use fir resin instead of wax to seal any spell involving words written on folded pieces of paper, or in place of glue in magical crafts. And of course, fir is a perfect tree for use in Yule/Winter Solstice celebrations!

✦ MAGICAL ASSOCIATIONS ✦

GENDER: Feminine

ELEMENT: Earth

PLANET: Moon, Jupiter, Pluto

ZODIAC: Capricorn, Cancer

DEITIES: Osiris, Artemis, Diana, the Triple Goddess

Hawthorn

(*CRATAEGUS* SPP.)

Range of native habitat: Temperate regions of the Northern Hemisphere

Hawthorn is a smaller tree, often appearing as a bush but capable of growing to heights of between 30 and 40 feet (9–12 m). There are several hundred species. It produces white flowers in spring and bright red-purple berries in autumn, and it has sharp thorns growing from its branches or trunk. In prior centuries, the thorns made it a favorite for growing in hedgerows to keep out thieves. Hawthorn leaves are generally oval-shaped but in some species more closely resemble oak leaves.

Hawthorn was associated with marriage across cultures in ancient Europe. In parts of Greece, newly married couples wore crowns with the blossoms, while the other celebrants carried torches made from the branches. In the British Isles, the couples would dance around a hawthorn tree to bless their union. The tree had another highly important function as the official signal of the start of summer and thus the time for Beltane celebrations. (Hawthorn blossoms in May, and in the years prior to the adoption of the Gregorian calendar, this typically occurred at the start of the month.) The blossoms were woven into crowns and garlands worn by the Beltane revelers. Hawthorn is also known as the May Tree, and was incorporated into May Day celebrations as the tree used for the maypole.

Hawthorn was also the subject of many taboos and other folk beliefs. Along with oak and ash, hawthorn is one of the faerie triad, meaning that wherever these three trees grow together, the faeries are likely to dwell. A lone hawthorn is perhaps even more enchanted, as it was believed to mark the boundary between the material and faerie worlds, especially if found near a well or spring. Harming such a tree in any way could bring severe misfortune. Furthermore, while hawthorn branches could be used to decorate the yard for the summer festivities, it was taboo to bring it into the house, which was said to risk illness and death. Hawthorn also symbolized death for some Germanic tribes, who used the wood in funeral pyres.

Hawthorn's medicinal properties are found in the flowers, leaves, berries, and bark, and are used by healers for circulatory disorders, migraines, sore throats, and menopausal symptoms. The flowers and bark are also used as sedatives. The berries contain vitamins B and C, and can be made (along with the blossoms) into wine and jelly. Hawthorn leaves are also edible. Note that hawthorn can interact with medications used for heart disease, so if you have a heart condition, definitely consult your physician before using.

Magically, hawthorn is used in workings related to fertility, purity, marriage, protection, patience, confidence, and creativity. The tree essence promotes forgiveness and love, releasing negativity from the heart center, making hawthorn an excellent tree for healing issues in a marriage. Use the blossoms in early summer in spellwork related to finding a serious romantic partner. Use the berries in fertility magic.

Hawthorn's protective properties work particularly well against negative psychic vibrations, and, like holly, it is also thought to protect against lightning. Placing hawthorn outside near doors and windows guards against unwanted influences, as does growing it in a hedge. Hawthorn is also a purifier, used in smudge sticks to energetically clear new houses, sacred space, and rooms where a person has been ill.

Wands of hawthorn are excellent for magic related to creativity and self-confidence, and for gaining insight into a complex situation. Workings related to weather, happiness, good luck, and breaking unwanted habits also benefit from hawthorn's energies. Add the flowers, berries, or bark shavings to sachets and other charms for these purposes. Try using the thorns to carve symbols into candles in lieu of a crystal point or pin, particularly in a spell relating to any of hawthorn's magical associations.

✦ MAGICAL ASSOCIATIONS ✦

GENDER: Feminine
ELEMENT: Water, Air, Earth
PLANET: Mars
ZODIAC: Taurus, Cancer
DEITIES: Hera, Flora, Venus, Olwen, Brigid

Holly

(*ILEX* SPP.)

Range of native habitat: Temperate and tropical zones worldwide

Ilex is a large and very widespread genus, with over four hundred species of trees and shrubs found in many different places around the world. American holly grows naturally in shaded woods and on the banks of streams and rivers, but various species of holly are also cultivated as hedges around homes and estates.

A cheerful plant whether in shrub, hedge, or tree form, holly is a symbol of luck, good fortune, and eternal life. Holly has always been particularly appreciated in northern climates, where its bright green leaves and red berries provide some much-needed color in the otherwise white and gray landscapes of wintertime. In some places, predictions about the coming winter were made based on the numbers of holly berries emerging on the trees. If there were more berries than usual, a colder, harder winter was expected.

Holly was also viewed as a protective tree and therefore a tree not to be cut down or burned. (However, harvesting boughs for decoration was allowed.) In particular, holly protected against bad luck, evil spirits, and lightning, and was therefore a desirable tree to plant near one's home. It is now believed that the holly leaves themselves, with their prickly spines, may act as conductors of lightning, drawing the electricity away from nearby objects.

The Druids revered holly (see pages 24–25) and used it for decoration at the Winter Solstice and during the winter months. It was said that bringing holly into the home was an invitation to the faeries (presumably the good ones!) to come in and shelter from the cold. The energy of the holly kept the faeries and the humans comfortably out of each other's way in the cozy, small space. In Scotland, people placed holly branches outside the house to keep evil at bay. Holly was also important to the Norse. It was associated with Thor, the god of thunder and lightning, and in some myths it is said that Odin's sacred spear was made of holly. The ancient Romans celebrated Saturnalia with boughs of holly, giving them as gifts to their friends.

One species of holly from the Brazilian rainforest (*Ilex paraguariensis*) provides the leaves for yerba mate, a naturally caffeinated tea that many find to be uplifting to the spirit. However, many species of holly are poisonous to humans. and the berries in particular are dangerous to children. This may be why holly's medicinal properties are rarely employed by modern herbalists, but we do know that the leaves and bark were used among Native Americans as an emetic (to induce vomiting) and to heal psychological and emotional imbalances.

The flower and tree essences of holly help to dispel negative emotions like jealousy and the desire for revenge, and to give support to the process of opening the heart and restoring peace of mind. Holly can be used in magic related to balancing emotions and finding balance in the midst of busy days, reenergizing during the dark days of winter, and victory over challenging situations. It is also effective in workings for love, attraction, and fertility, and can be carried in a sachet by men who wish to attract women. The leaves and berries make useful allies in any spellwork, whether as active ingredients or as energetic assistants on the altar.

If you're looking to plant a hedge around the perimeter of your property, holly creates a strong yet attractive protective shield.

Planting a holly tree creates a faerie-friendly yard and a place to spend time communing with the Otherworld. Bring boughs of holly into the house for Yule celebrations, and then burn the dried greens at Imbolc to welcome in the new growing season.

GENDER: Masculine, Feminine

ELEMENT: Fire

PLANET: Mars, Saturn

ZODIAC: Leo, Sagittarius

DEITIES: Lugh, Thor, Mars, Gofannon, Goibniu

Maple

(*Acer* spp.)

Range of native habitat: Asia, Europe, northern Africa, North America

Maples have distinctly shaped leaves and are one of the few deciduous trees with an opposite branching arrangement, meaning that the leaves and buds grow directly across from each other on each side of the stem, rather than alternating up the sides. There are more than one hundred species of maple, with varying height ranges.

Although maples are native to Europe, European pagan traditions seem not to have viewed maple as a go-to magical tree. However, to anyone who has witnessed maple's annual display of stunningly vivid leaf coloring or tasted the sweetness of pure maple syrup, it's clear that Nature imbued this lovely tree with plenty of magic. In fact, the five-pointed leaves of some species of maple are even reminiscent of the star inside the pentacle, a symbol much revered by Wiccans and other Witches. And the annual cycle of the sugar maple, whose sap runs in the spring and whose leaves flame gloriously before leaving the branches bare for winter, makes for an excellent living symbol of the Wheel of the Year.

On a symbolic level, maple has been said to stand for generosity, abundance, success, balance, and practicality. Maple has medicinal uses, too; the inner bark has been used to treat mild coughs and digestive issues, while treatments for sore eyes have been created from the bark and the sap. Maple leaves can be packed around apples and root vegetables to help preserve them into the colder months. Maple tree essence assists with finding balance, self-sufficiency, and unconditional love of life.

The syrup of the sugar, red, or black maple is perhaps the most well known and widely accessible magical ingredient that maple provides. Used in kitchen witchery for love and money magic, maple syrup also has the advantage of being a healthier and more nutritious alternative to sugar. This underscores one of maple's subtle spiritual messages—that it's bene-ficial for us to allow sweetness and joy into our lives. Use maple syrup in magic for attracting love, mending a strained rela-tionship, or soothing a troubled mind. Or charm an entire bottle of it for a "prosperity syrup" that you can use daily on pancakes, in smoothies, and so on. Just be sure to check the label before you buy, as much of what is sold as maple syrup in grocery stores is just flavored corn syrup. (Hint: If it's cheap, it's probably not real maple syrup.)

Maple has been called the traveler's wood, perhaps because it was used by many indigenous North American tribes to make paddles and oars. Add a small twig or strip of maple bark to a travel charm for extra luck and comfort. A wand of maple is ideal for those who are constantly on the move, as well as those who appreciate beauty, harmony, and storytelling. Many musical instruments are made from maple wood, going back at least as far as the Anglo-Saxon period in Britain, which illustrates maple's association with beauty and harmony. Use the leaves, twigs, or bark in any spellwork centered on drawing these qualities into your life. Maple is also useful in magical workings related to intellectual pursuits, communication, and decisions, especially those involving a change in your situation.

✦ MAGICAL ASSOCIATIONS ✦

GENDER: Feminine, Masculine
ELEMENT: Spirit, Water, Earth
PLANET: Moon, Jupiter, Neptune
ZODIAC: Libra, Virgo
DEITIES: Danu, Hera, any lunar goddess

Oak

(*QUERCUS* SPP.)

Range of native habitat: Cool temperate to tropical regions of the Northern Hemisphere

There are approximately five hundred species of oak, one of the most majestic trees in the Northern Hemisphere. Its graceful, wide-reaching branches create an impressive canopy of distinctly shaped leaves, and it can reach heights of between 80 and 100 feet (24–30 m). Often the canopy is nearly as wide as the height of the tree. The oak tree's size and longevity (some species live an average of three hundred years), along with the many benefits it provides to humans and animals alike, have led it to be considered the king of the forest in many cultures. It is also

a beloved symbol of the Hermetic principle of "as above, so below," since its underground root system tends to mirror the spread of its branches.

In Rome, the mighty oak was symbolic of military strength, and victorious military leaders wore crowns of oak leaves when celebrating their wins. Oak was associated with powerful leader gods across several cultures, including Greek, Roman, Celtic, and ancient Germanic deities. It was also associated with gods of thunder and lightning, perhaps due to its propensity to be struck by lightning and, often enough, survive to grow even taller and wider. The Druids, who held their rituals in oak groves, believed that the mistletoe found in some oak trees was left there by divine lightning strikes. The Druids were also known to eat acorns as part of their divination practices.

Oak was important to our pagan ancestors in both magical and more mundane realms. Early settlers in Britain, as well as their livestock, were kept fed by acorns, and oak wood was highly useful for building housing and furniture as well as a consistent source of firewood. Folk traditions of the British Isles held that oak had magical healing abilities, and some believed that walking around the trunk of a living oak would cure what ailed them, as the first bird to alight on the tree afterward would carry off their sickness. A widely known folk custom holds that catching a falling oak leaf in autumn will protect you from colds and flu all winter long.

Oak bark has been used medicinally as an astringent to treat bowel issues, fever, sore throat, inflamed gums, eczema, bruises, and aches. One treatment for frostbite called for boiling oak leaves that had wintered over while still attached to the tree. Acorns are rich in B vitamins, calcium, and potassium and they are believed to improve metabolism, support bone health, and help prevent diabetes. Do not use oak bark if you have heart issues.

Magically, oak is symbolic of strength, prosperity, and fertility. Its longevity and ability to survive hardships such as lightning, drought, and fire also evoke the qualities of courage, wisdom, and endurance. It is excellent for workings related to wisdom in authority, personal sovereignty, protection, longevity, abundance, and fertility, as well as finding the truth in confusing situations.

Oak's magic can be harnessed from its bark, timber, leaves, and acorns. Use the bark in incense and sachets, or carry it in your wallet or purse for protection, abundance, and fertility. Burn the leaves for purification, or use them in healing and protection spells or any working involving victory. Wear a leaf on a ribbon or in a charm bag around your neck (under your shirt) to be able to perceive when others are being untruthful. Add a few leaves to your bath for healing emotional issues and gaining strength and fortitude to deal with challenges.

Acorns are instant magical charms in and of themselves. Charge them and keep them in your pocket, or add them to sachets and witch jars for any purpose, but especially for prosperity, wealth, fertility, and protection from illness. It is said that acorns are best gathered at night for fertility work, and planted during the Dark Moon for prosperity. Place them in windowsills to protect the home and attract good fortune.

Oak is one of the most energetically radiant trees, and ideal for meditating under and attuning to the spirits within it. Connect with an oak to help find focus in the midst of distractions or when you're seeking comfort from the benevolent energies of Mother Nature.

✦ MAGICAL ASSOCIATIONS ✦

GENDER: Masculine

ELEMENT: Water, Earth, Air, Spirit

PLANET: Jupiter, Mars, Sun

ZODIAC: Leo

DEITIES: Hecate, Pan, Zeus, Rhea, Diana, Jupiter, Herne, Cernunnos, Brigid, the Dagda, the Green Man

Pine

(*PINUS* SPP.)

Range of native habitat: Northern Hemisphere, some tropic and temperate regions of the Southern Hemisphere

The genus *Pinus* is a plentiful one, with 126 species of trees covering a wide range of habitats. Pines grow in the Arctic as well as in the desert and the tropics, so it's safe to assume that anyone anywhere wishing to connect magically with a pine will have little trouble finding one. Typically, pines are tall, coniferous evergreens, with heights averaging between 50 and 80 feet (15–24 m). They are recognizable from other conifers by their bundles of long, needle-like leaves and generally larger cones.

Sacred to the Druids and many native North American peoples, the pine tree has plenty of history, lore, and magical traditions on both sides of the Atlantic. Pine is listed among the seven "Nobles of the Wood" in medieval Irish records and is considered a symbol of peace among the Iroquois tribes. Some species of pine are extremely long lived, as we can see from the bristlecone pines in California, which are nearly five thousand years old. Pines are also quite hardy—they even survived the last Ice Age in some places and were among the first plants to flourish afterward. Perhaps the Druids, who burned pine at the winter solstice and decorated live pine trees with shiny objects, were aware of the strength and resilience of this mighty evergreen.

Pine needles have been used medicinally to relieve congestion and heal kidney and bladder issues. A bath made with the needles and cones can help with breathing and skin problems. (Note: Those with sensitive skin might become irritated from a pine bath.) Essential oil of pine is also helpful for clearing the sinuses and relieving sore muscles and joints, and it has antiviral and antiseptic properties. (Note: Be cautious with this oil, as it can irritate the skin and mucous membranes.) Pine oil has an uplifting and energizing effect in aromatherapeutic applications and it is useful in cleaning products. Nutritionally, pine is prized for its needles, which contain vitamin C, and its seeds (known as pine nuts), which contain vitamin E, magnesium, and potassium. The nuts are also delicious in pesto!

Symbolically, pine represents immortality, rebirth, health, fertility, strength (especially during hard times), and prosperity. It is used magically for purification, protection, fertility, renewal, longevity, and good fortune. Use a wand of pine in ritual and spellwork for any of these purposes, or in magic that uses only gestures and no spoken words. Attach a pine cone to the tip of any wand to enhance divine masculine energy and fertility. Carry pine cones to increase healthy longevity as well as fertility (pine nuts, needles, and bark also work for fertility). For protection, burn pine needles in the fire. Place a pine branch over your bed to keep illness away. To banish negativity from any space, burn pine incense or essential oil, or use pine oil in a cleaning solution for floors, walls, or laundry. You can also use a pine branch as a besom to sweep out negative energy from indoor or outdoor spaces. A purification bath with pine needles raises energy and fosters clarity over troubling issues, as does meditating at the base of a pine tree. Use pine nuts in kitchen witchery for increased prosperity, and hang a pine branch over your front door to maintain good fortune.

GENDER: Masculine, Feminine

ELEMENT: Air, Fire, Earth, Spirit

PLANET: Mars, Jupiter, Saturn

ZODIAC: Cancer, Capricorn

DEITIES: Isis, Artemis, Pan, Ariadne, Rhea, Diana, Dionysus

Rowan (Mountain Ash)

(*SORBUS* SPP.)

Range of native habitat: Cool-temperate Northern Hemisphere

Rowan is often referred to as mountain ash, particularly in North America, due to its smooth bark, upward-reaching branches, and compound leaves, which are similar to those of ash. However, the two are not botanically related, and rowan is typically a much shorter tree, reaching average heights of 10 to 30 feet (3–9 m). The "mountain" descriptor comes from rowan's ability to grow at high elevations and endure harsh conditions; it often sprouts up from cracks between rocks where birds have dropped seeds from the berries. The elevations at which they can grow and the bright red hues of its berries may have been what led some ancient Celts to believe that rowan provided food for the Aos Sí, the faerie race.

Rowan's status as a magical tree may also be due in part to the unique five-pointed star appearing on each of its red berries, a symbol of protection in many ancient traditions. For the Celts, rowan was particularly associated with protection from negative magic, of both human and faerie origins. Rowans were planted near the front door of homes to protect the house and all who dwelled within. Rowan wood was used to kindle fires to protect cattle from faeries. Sprigs were hung at Beltane above doorways, children's cradles, and butter churns (to keep the faeries from spoiling the butter). Protective charms were made from its twigs.

Druids used the rowan for magical craft, ritual, and divination. The bark and berries were used to dye ritual garments, and the wood for funeral fires. Ceremonial cakes were cooked over fires of rowan wood. Twigs were used for divining for metals and were crushed into incense for use in divination. Rowan was considered so sacred in Scotland that its wood was traditionally never used for anything but ritual purposes.

The Scandinavians also saw rowan as protective and planted trees near their farm buildings to secure protection for crops and animals against storms and other damage. Rowans that grew in the most unlikely or inaccessible places were considered to be the most powerful and were referred to as "flying rowan." The tree was sacred to Thor because it once saved him from drowning in a river by bending over so he could grab hold of it. In some translations of Norse mythology it is the rowan, rather than the elm, that the first woman was made from.

Some contemporary Norse pagan traditions hold that the ancient rune masters used rowan branches to carve runes for divination. Interestingly, the English word *rowan* shares its origin with the Old Norse word *runa*, which translates to "a secret" or "to whisper."

Rowan berries contain large amounts of vitamin C and were used to prevent and treat scurvy. Ripe berries were used for their diuretic and purgative properties, and the bark was used to soothe upset stomachs. The berries have also been made into wine, ale, spirits, and jelly; they contain an acid that is toxic when they are raw (do *not* eat the berries raw, as it can cause serious complications, including kidney damage) but becomes safe once the berries are cooked. There are numerous medications that interact with the berries and cause harm to the kidneys, so talk to your health care provider before consuming rowan berries.

Magically, rowan is still used today in workings related to protection, psychic ability and insight, healing, and positivity. It is still planted in yards to protect the home from negative vibrations and to bring the blessing of the faeries. To make a traditional protection charm, place two rowan twigs in an equal-armed cross and secure it with red thread. Keep one in your home and bring one with you when traveling.

Rowan berries are specifically useful in amulets and charm bags for strength, power, and healing. The tree's hardiness makes it a symbol of beauty, grace, and perseverance in the face of challenges. Rowan is also excellent for workings related to psychic perception and attunement to Nature. Add rowan bark to incense to burn during divination, and hold a wand or staff (or walking stick) of rowan while hiking through the forest to connect more deeply with the spirits and energies of the forest. Meditate under a rowan tree to strengthen your ability to hear your inner wisdom. If you don't have access to rowan trees, the tree essence can have similar effects.

GENDER: Masculine

ELEMENT: Fire

PLANET: Sun, Mercury, Uranus

ZODIAC: Aquarius

DEITIES: Hebe, Pan, Thor, Herne, Brigid, Lugh, the Crone

Willow

(*SALIX* SPP.)

Range of native habitat: Cold and temperate regions of the Northern Hemisphere

The genus *Salix* contains over four hundred species of trees and shrubs and is widespread in the Northern Hempisphere, from stately trees to ones on the smaller side. Willows typically have narrow, elongated leaves; slender branches; and soft, pliant wood. The most well-known species is probably the weeping willow, which is native to Asia and found as an ornamental tree in many parks, gardens, and yards.

The word *willow* shares linguistic roots with the word *witch* in ancient Indo-European languages, and indeed the tree itself has been associated with both Moon and Crone goddesses among the ancient Greeks, Romans, and Celts alike. The Greek mythical poet Orpheus was said to have received his creative gifts after touching the willows in a sacred grove, and he carried willow branches with him as he traveled through the Underworld. Willows growing near wells were sometimes turned into "wishing trees" in Celtic areas,

particularly when the wish
was for healing from the
grief of a broken heart.

The willow's con-
nections with wisdom,
mystery, death, and
the afterlife seem to go
back to prehistoric times.
This may be at least in part
because willows are often
found near water, which in
turn links this tree with the
Moon. The afterlife asso-
ciation may also be due
to willow's regenerative
abilities—a cut branch planted
in the ground can quickly grow into a
new tree. In Celtic myth, the willow also plays an important role in
creation itself—it was in a willow tree that two scarlet snake eggs
were hidden, one containing the Sun and the other containing the
Earth, until the eggs hatched and the full cosmos came into being.

In the medicinal realm, willow is best known for a component in
its bark called salicin, which is the primary ingredient in aspirin.
Prior to the invention of aspirin, young willow twigs were chewed
for pain relief. The bark has also been used to treat rheumatism,
colds, and fever. Willow sap can be used to reduce acne, and the
leaves and bark can be boiled and used as a treatment for dandruff.

In the magical realm, willow is symbolic of renewal and immortality, again due to its ability to regenerate from a broken branch.
It is also associated with resolving or healing grief, as its "otherworldly" yet reassuring energy reminds us that we are all eternal
beings. Due to its quick rate of growth, willow also assists with

magic concerning vitality, and its association with the Moon makes it excellent for workings related to cyclical change. In fact, willow is good for all Moon-related magic in any phase of the lunar cycle.

Use willow in spells, rituals, or other workings related to letting go of relationships and old hurts, accepting loss, and making way for renewal in the form of new blessings coming into your life. Willow can also be used in spells for love and healing. Crush the leaves and bark to use in incense for these purposes, or charm a piece of bark to carry with you until your goal has manifested.

Willow makes good dowsing wands for finding water. Furthermore, it is said that willow's wood naturally aligns with the energy raised in magical work, making it an excellent choice for wands in general, and especially for those just starting out in the Craft. Willow's watery, lunar properties also make it ideal for workings related to psychic ability, divination, and astral travel. Try placing three willow leaves under your pillow for clear, informative dreams. Sit under a willow tree and meditate or write in your journal about an issue that's been troubling you—especially matters of the heart—and ask the spirit of the tree for guidance.

✦ MAGICAL ASSOCIATIONS ✦

GENDER: Feminine

ELEMENT: Water

PLANET: Moon

ZODIAC: Cancer, Scorpio

DEITIES: Persephone, Hera, Hecate, Ceres, Artemis, Selene, Luna, Diana, Minerva, Cerridwen, Brigid, Arianrhod, Rhiannon, the Morrigan

Yew

(*TAXUS* SPP.)

Range of native habitat: Temperate zones of the Northern Hemisphere

There are only eight species of yew trees. Two of the species are shrubby, but some of the others can reach up to 80 feet (24 m) tall. All have dark green foliage with flattish, linear leaves

Yew is highly significant in the lore of our ancestors in the Craft. Among magical trees, it has perhaps one of the most mysterious energies. This may be due in part to its capacity to live for several thousand years, but also its unusual ability to "rebirth" itself. It can send aerial roots into its own decaying heartwood and form new trunks, which then emerge from within the hollowed-out central trunk of the original tree. This phenomenon makes it difficult to tell a given yew's age, since the tree rings of the original trunk are destroyed by the new growth. However, one particularly ancient yew found in Scotland has been estimated to be at least five thousand years old. It should come as no surprise that the yew has been associated since ancient times with longevity, rebirth, regeneration, and reincarnation by the Greeks, Celts, and Germanic peoples alike.

The ancient Irish Celts understood the mighty longevity of the yew, and it was considered to be one of the oldest living beings on the Earth. Irish mythology tells us that yew was brought to the Emerald Isle from the Otherworld, one of five sacred trees that helped establish the ancient kingdoms of Ireland. It was also named as one of the Seven Chieftain Trees of Brehon law in pre-Christian Ireland, so anyone trimming a yew risked bad luck and even punishment. Yew was seen as a symbol of death and resurrection, and the leaves were placed on graves to affirm that a new life awaited the recently departed.

The Germanic peoples also revered the yew, associating it with the Winter Solstice as well as with death and rebirth. The ancient runes Eihwaz and Yr represented both the tree and its regenerative powers. In fact, several old European names for yew can be traced back etymologically to words meaning "eternal," showing that the timeless quality of the yew has always been recognized. Yews are also well known in Europe for their presence in ancient churchyards, particularly in the British Isles, many of which are presumed to predate Christianity. While some of these trees may indeed have been planted during Christian times, many are likely traceable to pagan days, when yews marked sacred spaces and portals to the underworld.

Yews are extremely toxic and therefore not used medicinally, with one exception—a prescription drug derived from yew bark that was used to treat breast and ovarian cancer (the drug is now manufactured in a lab). Aside from this, yew is not physically beneficial to humans. Magically, however, yew is a powerful ally. It can assist with workings related to knowledge, wisdom, spiritual growth, protection, transformation, psychic abilities, strength, and rebirth. A branch of yew makes for an excellent wand or even dowsing rod and can be held in your hands to enhance spirit communication and astral travel. Many who work with runes or the Ogham for divination purposes love to carve these symbols into small yew twigs, as yew has been associated with divination and shamanic mysteries in both Druid and Norse traditions. (Just be sure to keep such items away from children or pets who may be tempted to chew on them!)

Yew has a reputation for being a tree "between worlds"; some believe this may be because the tree emits a hallucinogenic gas—although it has not been thoroughly researched—on warm days. If you have access to a yew tree, you might try meditating near it on a warm sunny afternoon. (Depending on your sensitivity, you might want to have someone to check in with you at an agreed-upon time, just to make sure you don't overdo it.) If you don't live near any yew trees, you can still call upon its mystical properties through visualization or focusing on an image of a yew. For help in releasing a difficult situation, imagine re-rooting your life path with the branches of your current circumstances. What "failures" or "deaths" have you experienced that could be regenerated into something new and positive?

✦ MAGICAL ASSOCIATIONS ✦

GENDER: Feminine

ELEMENT: Earth, Water

PLANET: Saturn, Pluto, Jupiter

ZODIAC: Scorpio

DEITIES: Artemis, Persephone, Hecate, Odin, Banbha, the Morrigan, the Crone

GATHERING AND GROWING
MAGICAL FLOWERS

THE LIFESPAN OF FLOWERS IS FLEETING, BUT THEY CAN BE more accessible than trees to work magic with, especially for those who live in apartments and urban areas. You can't exactly bring a tree into your home (unless it's a small, indoor ornamental variety), but you can bring in garden flowers and wildflowers during the summer, or bouquets from the supermarket all year round—and brighten up your home while you're at it. If you're lucky enough to have the time and space, a flower garden is an excellent way to attune with the energies of these special plants.

Witches typically prefer to grow and gather flowers native to where they live, as this is a great way of staying in harmony with the energies of Nature. While it's wonderful that we can grow exotic flowers from all over the world if we want to, we've also learned that bringing in species from other continents can wreak havoc on ecosystems they are not indigenous to, causing harm to other plant and animal life (this can be easily witnessed in the American South, where trees are regularly swallowed by Asian vines like kudzu and nonnative wisteria). So when it comes to working with flowers, the advice of this guide is to think globally by growing locally.

Gathering flowers from the wild for magical work is a time-honored tradition that puts us in mind of our pagan ancestors foraging in the meadows and forests for their ritual Beltane crowns. But roadsides and even your backyard may offer up some great magical allies for your spellwork. Just make sure to leave plenty of blooming flowers for the bees and other pollinators to work their own magic in co-creating the food supply and keeping ecosystems healthy. Keep in mind also that many indigenous species are endangered, whether due to habitat loss or the introduction of nonnative plants, especially those considered to be invasive. Before you go flower gathering, learn to identify any endangered flowers in your area so you'll know to leave them in place.

In fact, you should always stick with what you know and recognize when it comes to harvesting from Nature. If something looks unfamiliar, it's best to leave it be. This will help you avoid picking something that's endangered and, equally important, help you avoid rashes and other unwanted reactions to toxic plants. Take time to learn how to recognize poison ivy, poison oak, poison sumac, and giant hogweed, and always wear gloves and long sleeves if there's a chance you'll come across them. There are many plant recognition apps that can help you identify nearly any kind of plant simply by snapping a picture and uploading it. These are worthwhile investments for any nature-loving Witch!

If you have the space and the inclination, growing flowers of your own is a great way to really connect with the energies of Nature. Grow them from bulbs, seeds, or starter plants in pots or garden beds. Work with native flowering plants to tune in to the natural energies of your particular area (not to mention the fact that they're typically the easiest to grow). Many cultivated varieties of native flowers (sometimes called nativars, a twist on the word *cultivar*) are also available as seeds and starter plants; these flowers can offer more variety of color and size than their indigenous counterparts.

Yet there are ecological considerations to take with nativars as well. First, these flowers may not be as useful for pollinators as their native counterparts. Some are even inaccessible to bees due to their modified shapes and structures. When choosing nativars to grow in your garden, find out which ones are the most pollinator-friendly. Nativars can also negatively impact the genetic diversity of the ecosystems where they're grown, potentially hybridizing with their wild counterparts in the surrounding area, which can weaken the wild version of the plant. Much is still unknown about the cumulative impact of nativars on a given ecosystem, as each species and each cultivated variety of that species is different. (When it comes to indoor flowering plants, of course, native ecology isn't an issue, so feel free to grow whatever exotic species you like in your home.)

MAGICAL ASSOCIATIONS
FOR COMMON WILDFLOWERS

NEARLY ALL OF THE FLOWERS IN THIS WITCH'S DOZEN ARE found as wildflowers in North America, as either native or naturalized species (nonnative plants that have integrated without being invasive). Daffodils are the exception, as they only grow from planted bulbs, but they can be found "wild" in some natural areas that were reclaimed from previously settled lands. Most of these also have European counterparts and thus have long traditions of folklore and magical use. Coneflowers (*Echinacea* spp.) and sunflowers are not native to Europe, but they have been used in North American indigenous plant medicine and magic for thousands of years.

The flower colors listed on the following table are the most common colors occurring in native species. However, flowers may come in other colors, depending on the area you live in. Many are also available as cultivars in several additional colors.

COMMON WILDFLOWERS AND THEIR MAGICAL ASSOCIATIONS

FLOWER	SCIENTIFIC NAME	NATIVE HABITAT
BUTTERCUP	*Ranunculus* spp.	North America, Europe
COLUMBINE	*Aquilegia* spp.	Northern Hemisphere
CONEFLOWER	*Echinacea* spp.	Eastern and central North America
DAFFODIL	*Narcissus* spp.	Southern Europe and North Africa
DAISY	(1) *Bellis perennis* or (2) *Leucanthemum vulgare*	(1) Europe, naturalized in most temperate regions; (2) Europe, temperate regions of Asia
FOXGLOVE	*Digitalis* spp.	Europe, western Asia, northwestern Africa
GERANIUM	(1) *Geranium maculatum* or (2) *Pelargonium* spp.	(1) North American woodland; (2) Warm temperate and tropical regions worldwide
HONEYSUCKLE	*Lonicera* spp.	Northern latitudes of North America and Eurasia

COLOR(S)	MAGICAL ASSOCIATIONS	SPECIAL NOTES
Yellow	Love, commitment, fertility, fidelity, humility	Some species are poisonous to humans and pets.
Purple, pink, red, and yellow	Love, feminine power, beauty, courage	Roots and seeds are poisonous to humans and pets.
Yellow, purple	Strength, protection from illness, resilience, prosperity	
White, yellow	New beginnings, peace, love, fertility, luck	Poisonous to humans and pets.
Mainly white and yellow	Youthful energy, joy, love, flirtation, baby blessings	Some species can be poisonous to humans and pets.
Mainly purple; also white, pink, yellow	Protection, clairvoyance, communication with faeries	Poisonous to humans and pets. Considered invasive in some areas of North America.
White, pink, blue, purple	Happiness, healing, overcoming negativity, fertility, childbirth, protection	*Pelargonium* spp. is toxic to animals.
White, pink, red, orange, yellow	Intuition, psychic ability, prosperity, love, luck	

FLOWER	SCIENTIFIC NAME	NATIVE HABITAT
LILAC	*Syringa* spp.	Southeastern Europe to eastern Asia; widely cultivated in temperate regions elsewhere
MARIGOLD	*Tagetes* spp.	Southwestern United States into South America
SNAPDRAGON	*Antirrhinum majus*	Southern Europe, Mediterranean region
SUNFLOWER	*Helianthus annuus*	North America
VIOLET	*Viola* spp.	Temperate regions of the Northern Hemisphere

COLOR(S)	MAGICAL ASSOCIATIONS	SPECIAL NOTES
Mainly purple; also white, pink	Psychic ability, divination, banishing negativity, wisdom, memory	Actually a shrub or tree.
White, yellow, orange, red	Psychic ability, healing from grief, love, protection	Mildly poisonous to humans and animals.
Mainly red; also white, pink, yellow	Protection, repelling negative energy, purification, clear thinking, strength	
Mainly yellow and brown; also orange, red	Success, good health, happiness, wisdom, positive energy	
Mainly blue; also white, yellow, purple	Protection, love, restful sleep, tranquility, harmony, luck	

CONNECTING WITH NATURE SPIRITS

WHEN IT COMES TO WORKING WITH THE NONPHYSICAL spiritual energies of Nature, magic is all about connection. Many modern Wiccan and other magical traditions make much of "working with the faeries." But, as we saw in part 1, what is meant by *faeries* (or *fairies*, depending on your preferred spelling) can be different for each person. Many of the beings known in folklore as faeries were not always benevolent. Legends abound of faeries ruining crops, souring milk, and even stealing children. So before you go summoning or making offerings to "the faeries," get clear on just who you have in mind. There are plenty of stories of people who got unexpected (and often unwanted) results from simply calling on the faeries to see what would happen.

A wiser route is to get a feel for nature spirits first, by hanging out in Nature and learning from what you perceive. Trees, flowers, animals, and even bugs are physical embodiments of the spiritual energy that permeates all things, the energy that we are craving when we long to get out into the great outdoors. So start by connecting physically with the environment in order to connect with the spiritual plane.

Of course, not everyone has access to a forest or a mountain range, but it is extremely beneficial (and highly advised) to spend time in a natural setting to the extent that this is possible for you. If you're blessed with a yard that contains a tree or two, this is a great place to start. Otherwise, find a park, a greenway, or some other place where you can have access to a stream, a meadow, or at least a tree. You can bring a blanket to sit on and make it a picnic! For the best possible connection, sit or stand with your bare feet on the ground. And if you live anywhere near a forest with hiking trails, make a point of treating yourself to a hike every once in a while, even if it's just a short, easy walk.

Nature spirits may not make their presence known right away. Many humans have not given nature spirits a reason to be welcoming or willing to interact with them, so they are unlikely to trust you immediately. This is especially true in areas that have been disturbed by construction, fossil fuel extraction, litter, and pollution. So approach nature spirits with care and respect, and be patient until they trust you.

One way to demonstrate your trustworthiness is to pick up any trash in the area. Spirits appreciate any assistance in improving the quality of their home. Offerings of flowers, crystals, milk, honey, or small bits of food are also welcomed. Just make sure not to leave anything that could harm local wildlife, and offer only natural items. You can also speak to the energies of the land. Greet the trees, rocks, flowers, and sky and tell them how you appreciate them. Then quiet your mind and take time to simply observe the area, noticing as many details as you can. In time, you will begin to be aware of the spiritual plane at work all around you.

Gaze at the trunk or the canopy of a tree with a soft focus, and watch for faces to appear in the bark, leaves, or branches. Look also at the negative spaces around and between branches, as sometimes images appear in the dance between the canopy and the surrounding sky. Windy days are great for this form of scrying, as the leaves and branches may form moving pictures.

Wind itself is another method through which the Universe can communicate with you via trees. Have you ever watched a tree and noticed just two or three leaves fluttering in a breeze while the rest of the tree is still? Those micro currents of air are not merely air but gentle signals from the magical living energy of the tree itself. And if you're having an introspective moment near a tree and a sudden gust of wind shakes the leaves, consider what your most recent thought was—you might be getting confirmation of an idea or insight.

Note also the presence of animals around you. Animals can be easily influenced by unseen energy and so can be communicators of that energy. Learn to observe birds, squirrels, rabbits, and any other animals who make themselves known to you. These messengers are especially significant if they show up when you're contemplating a problem or thinking of departed loved ones.

As you develop your awareness of your environment, be alert for subtle changes in the energy of the place—in other words, how it feels to be there. Then do your best to work this practice of awareness and connection after you leave. Get in the habit of observing the trees and other plant life you pass on your way to work or school, whether it's grand evergreens along the highway, small ornamental maples outside a shopping center, or lilies in your neighbor's garden. Gently brush a leaf with your hand as you walk under a tree on the sidewalk, and give it a silent greeting. In the winter, take time to appreciate the shapes made by the bare branches of deciduous trees. Too often, these opportunities are lost in the fast pace of our modern world. Make a point of integrating these small moments into your daily life.

BRANCHING OUT

NOW THAT YOU'VE BEEN INTRODUCED TO SOME OF THE MOST common magical trees and flowers in North America, you can begin connecting with them both physically and metaphysically—through meditation, visualization, and spellwork. In part 3, you'll find a diverse collection of ideas and magical workings to inspire and develop your practice: connecting with Nature on the astral plane, making your own wand, and spells for love, abundance, and protection. Enjoy these offerings and, as always, go where your intuition leads you!

PART THREE

NATURE RITUALS, SPELLS, AND CRAFTS

A GRIMOIRE FOR THE
GREAT OUTDOORS

WORKING WITH THE MAGICAL GIFTS OF THE NATURAL world is a beautifully rewarding way to practice the Craft, wherever you're communing with Nature: in a forest, in a grove, in a park, in your backyard, or at your indoor altar. The spells, rituals, and other workings offered here consist almost exclusively of tree and flower ingredients. Many call for hand-gathering leaves, bark, flowers, and so on. However, if you want to work with a tree or flower that doesn't grow in your area, you can find many barks, branches, needles, cones, petals, and so on through online magical shops and herbal medicine suppliers. You can also look up the magical properties of other trees and flowers near you for appropriate substitutions.

ENCHANTED FOREST MEDITATION

THIS VISUALIZATION EXERCISE IS A GREAT WAY TO UNWIND from a busy day, prepare yourself for magical work (especially tree magic!), or simply cultivate the habit of connecting with the energy of Nature. Here, you'll be going for an astral hike in the forest. If you don't have much personal experience with forests, you might want to spend some time looking at photographs or watching nature documentaries to get better acquainted with the kinds of imagery you can call up during the visualization. Exercises like these are good practice in co-creating with the Universe in the realm of imagination, for while you'll be creating your own individual forest in your mind's eye, you'll be allowing the details to come through to you from the astral plane.

Conducting a detailed meditation from written text can be a challenge, since you're unlikely to memorize every detail of the instructions before closing your eyes. Try learning the steps through listening: have a friend read the passage aloud, or record yourself reading it and then play it back. Another option is to copy down the instructions by hand, which will help you to remember them in better detail.

You might try enhancing the experience by playing actual forest sounds in the background (plenty of videos can be found online). And if you're not sure how much time to spend in the visualization, consider setting a timer for five, ten, or fifteen minutes.

The Visualization

Close your eyes and take a deep breath in. As you exhale, see the beginning of a path into the woods, marked by a sign that reads "Enchanted Forest." As you step onto the path, take another deep breath in. Slowly release the breath, allowing your mind to quiet a little. Now simply notice the scene in front of you. What trees are here? Look to the tops of the trees. How high up do the tallest ones reach? What can you see of the sky above? Now scan down slowly from the tops of the trees to the forest floor. What are the first visual details that call your attention? Allow the spirits of the forest to communicate with you through sight and sound, without trying to analyze the messages with the logical part of your brain.

What colors are dominant among the forest here? Notice the individual shades of brown and gray among the trunks of the trees. Is their bark ridged or smooth? What are the shapes of the leaves? What flowers do you see? What is the forest floor composed of? Are there fallen trees among the shrubs and other plants? Are there dead leaves slowly decaying and turning into soil?

Take another deep inhale through your nose and release it. What does the air smell like? What are the dominant scents your mind is experiencing right now?

What sounds are present? Listen to the sound of your own breath, and then let your audial awareness radiate out further. Listen for the breeze whispering through the leaves. Listen for the calls of birds from nearby and from deeper into the forest. Do you hear any small animals rustling along the forest floor?

Spend several moments here, simply attuning to the world you are co-creating. When you feel your analytical mind fading into the background and your perceptive mind emerging into your present awareness, begin walking along the path. As you step deeper into the forest, listen for the sounds of birds. Their calls and chirps are announcing your presence. Listen for rustling of leaves along the forest floor—these are small animals taking refuge from the vibrations of your footsteps. You are being noticed, and even watched, by the inhabitants of the forest. You are now, however temporarily, part of this magical ecosystem. Stay here as long as you like, or until the timer brings your awareness back to the room.

When you're finished with the visualization, consider trying out some new spellwork, writing in your journal, or engaging in some other creative activity. Feel free to return to your unique astral forest any time you wish.

You can also use this practice to develop astral connections with specific plant life that you don't have physical access to. For example, find several photographs of Pacific yews, and then spend time visualizing one of your own co-creation. You can then draw on the tree's subtle energies in your spellwork.

HARVESTING FROM TREES
FOR MAGICAL WORK

WHETHER YOU'RE LOOKING TO MAKE A WAND OR TO USE bark, leaves, flowers, and so on from a tree for spellwork, it is extremely important to go about the harvesting process carefully and respectfully. Cutting branches and bark from a tree creates an open wound that exposes the tree to bacteria, pests, mold, and so on and can compromise its ability to transport nutrients and water through the networks of its inner bark. Likewise, overharvesting spring blossoms or summer leaves can inhibit growth and interfere with natural processes like pollination and food production. For these and other reasons, many Witches prefer to leave a living tree alone and forage for blossoms, leaves, branches, and strips of bark that the tree has naturally shed. However, this doesn't mean that you can't ever harvest magical ingredients from a living tree—it just means that you need to be careful. Following the guidelines below and doing further research into the specific tree(s) you want to harvest from will help ensure that you don't overly disrupt the natural forces that you're seeking to work in harmony with.

DON'TS

✦ Don't cut bark from the trunk of a tree. This can severely compromise the tree's health. In fact, cutting just one strip of bark from the entire circumference of the trunk will likely kill the tree. Instead, remove a small branch (or twig) that you can reach easily, and then harvest the bark from the cut branch.

- ✦ Don't pull leaves off the tree by their stems, as this often also pulls off a bud that might otherwise grow into a new branch. Instead, cut a little way from the end of the stem.

- ✦ Don't use garden shears on trees. These can pinch the branch in a way that hinders healing and future growth.

- ✦ Don't harvest branches in damp weather, if possible, as this exposes the tree to more mold and bacteria than harvesting in dry weather.

- ✦ Don't take more than you need. Keep in mind the other living creatures that rely on the trees' blossoms, leaves, shade, and so on for their well-being.

DO'S

- ✦ Do research when the best time is to harvest the species you want to work with in terms of minimizing damage. For example, in four-season climates, spring is best for some trees, while fall is best for others. Work with the trees' natural rhythms as much as possible.

- ✦ Do use safe, appropriate cutting tools with caution. Keep blades sharp to avoid making ragged cuts that make it harder for the tree to heal. And be sure to clean your tools after harvesting to avoid spreading diseases among trees.

- ✦ Do cut branches as close to the base as you can and perpendicular to the branch collar (the joint where the branch attaches to the trunk, or to its parent branch).

- ✦ Do communicate respectfully and lovingly with the tree before, during, and after the harvesting process. See the following example ritual for a suggested approach that you can personalize.

A RITUAL FOR
HARMLESS HARVESTING

THIS SIMPLE RITUAL CAN BE TAILORED IN WHATEVER WAY suits your personal approach to magic. Just be sure to remember to respect, protect, and thank the tree. This process can also be adapted for harvesting flowers, if you like.

=== YOU WILL NEED ===

A cutting tool(s): a boline or other sharp knife, or a saw
(if harvesting larger branches)

A cloth bag or other container for the harvested items

An offering for the tree (see suggestions on page 114)

=== INSTRUCTIONS ===

Once you've identified the tree you'd like to work with, sit at the base of the tree (or as close as you can get). Greet the tree and talk to it for a little while. You might identify the things you appreciate about it—its graceful branches, smooth bark, bright leaves, and so on. (This is something you can do ahead of time or any time you come across a tree that seems to have a special energy about it. No need to limit your communications to just when you need something!) Talk about the spellwork you're preparing for, why you're working it, and what you wish to achieve.

When you feel ready, ask the tree's permission to harvest what you need. Sit in silence, breathing deeply, and listen with your intuitive mind for the answer. If you feel the tree is saying no, simply thank it for its response and move on. You can then find another tree and repeat the process. It's important that you honor the *no* rather than override it. The tree may be experiencing challenges to its overall health that would be exacerbated by your cutting something from it. Alternatively, it may be gently trying to tell you that you haven't thought your magical plans through sufficiently. If you keep getting a *no* from several trees, you may want to reevaluate the planned spell or even the goal itself.

If the tree does grant permission, take a deep breath in, and on the exhale visualize a protective white light infusing and surrounding the tree, so that it will not be harmed from your harvesting. Say the following (or similar) words:

With pure intentions and deepest love, I gratefully accept the gifts of this [name of tree]. *May the God and Goddess protect this* [name of tree] *from harm and keep it in good health. So let it be.*

Now, using your cutting instrument, harvest only what you need as quickly and cleanly as possible. Place the gathered material in the bag or other container, and close your eyes for a moment while you once more visualize the tree radiating with white light. See it in complete and vibrant health. Then say the following (or similar) words of thanks:

I give thanks to you, [name of tree], *and wish you health and vitality in all the seasons to come. Blessed be.*

Finally, leave an offering of some kind as a way of thanking the tree. There are many different traditions regarding what to leave for any given type of tree, but some of the more common offerings include small crystals, shiny new coins, a few splashes of wine or milk, small fruits, herbs, honey, and small handfuls of grain. Some Witches prefer to bring water or even fertilizer, which a tree can make use of. As with all things, follow your intuition.

TREE TRUNK GROUNDING RITUAL

GROUNDING, ALSO KNOWN AS EARTHING, IS A PRACTICE USED by Witches and modern alternative healers to reconnect the self with the physical body by connecting with the Earth. Grounding has positive effects on mental, physical, and spiritual health. There are many ways to accomplish grounding: the simple act of standing with your bare feet in the soil (or sand, if you're on a beach), lying on the ground, or various visualization processes that bring you into an awareness of your physical body, your connection to Earth, and the present moment. Grounding is used in Wiccan practice, both before and after rituals, to assist with focus during the ritual and transitioning back into ordinary reality afterward. The ceremony of cakes and ale is sometimes used as a grounding mechanism, as food helps settle practitioners back into their body after working with intense energies.

Trees provide a powerful resource for grounding, as they emanate a calming, healing presence and are perfect embodiments of being rooted in the Earth. This is also a great way to get acquainted with the energies of different species of trees, so you may want to work with a few and note your experiences in a journal to compare. For this ritual, it's ideal to be barefoot, but don't let that stop you from trying it in cold weather—you can keep your shoes on if need be.

Choose a tree with a reasonably large trunk that you can stand right next to. Stand in front of the tree trunk with both feet firmly planted on the ground. Place your receptive palm (your nondominant hand) against the tree trunk and hold it there for a few moments, breathing deeply. Notice the subtle changes in the energy of your body. Do you feel calmer? More enlivened? What shifts are taking place? Now, place your projective palm (your dominant hand) against the trunk, at least a couple of feet away from your other hand. Close your eyes. Visualize the energy of the tree entering through your receptive hand, traveling up through your arm and into your heart center. See it circulating throughout your heart center and slowly spreading throughout the rest of your body. Now see it traveling down through your other arm and exiting through your dominant hand back into the trunk of the tree. Stay there for a few more moments, breathing deeply, feeling the tree's energy humming throughout your body. When you're ready to release the energy, press both palms firmly into the trunk and silently thank the tree. (You can also give it a hug, if you feel comfortable.) Then take your hands away and shake your arms out gently to release any excess energy.

GREEN MAN/WOMAN LEAF CROWN

AUTUMN LEAVES PRESENT A WONDERFUL OPPORTUNITY TO work creatively with Nature in many ways. This magical headdress can be worn in celebration of Mabon or Samhain, depending on when peak leaf season hits your area. It's also a great costume for Witches who want to dress up for Halloween and express an aspect of their true selves at the same time. And it can be a fun project to do with kids! You can also make a summer version with just green leaves. Look for leaves and boughs that have come off due to wind, or snip some leaves (but first please review the information in "Harvesting from Trees for Magical Work," on pages 111–12).

The leaves need to have at least an inch of stem, so not all tree types will work, but oak and maple leaves in particular should be a safe bet. For best results, try to gather your leaves no more than three days before you plan to wear the headdress, and don't assemble it until the day you plan to wear it or the day before. Leaves begin to lose their vitality once they've left the tree, so the longer they sit, the less vibrant and pliable they will appear in the finished piece. Note that the "crown" is actually made of separate pieces that you'll work into your hair, so your hair needs to be long enough to hold clips, bobby pins, or barrettes.

15–40 fresh autumn leaves
Twist ties or small rubber bands
1 or more large books (or other flat, smooth, heavy objects)
Several hair clips and/or bobby pins
1 or more candles (optional)
A mirror

══ INSTRUCTIONS ══

First, gather the leaves. If you're creating the autumn version, this can be the most enjoyable part of the process, as it requires you to start paying close attention to the colors of the trees as the season gets underway. This can be a great excuse for a trip to the park, the woods, or anywhere else that might provide a spectacular variety of leaves to choose from.

Look for the brightest, most blemish-free leaves you can find, and get as many different colors and shades as you can find. Include lots of red, orange, and yellow, but don't leave out greens or vibrant browns if you come across them. You'll need at least 15 leaves, but don't be afraid to gather more than you need (unless you're making a summer version and harvesting living leaves). The more you gather now, the better selection you'll have to choose from when you assemble the headdress.

Spread the leaves out on a table or the floor and sort them by color. For best results, sort them again by individual shades of color, as if you're creating a painter's palette. Identify any leaves that have blemishes, tears, or missing points and put them aside. (Depending on how many leaves you have left, you may want to do another round or two of culling—it's easy to get overenthusiastic during the gathering process!) If you like, you can use these leaves as seasonal altar decorations or return them to the Earth.

Create four to six leaf "bouquets" from the leaves that remain, using one or two leaves from each color pile. For best appearance, place all leaves faceup and arrange the biggest leaves at the back with smaller leaves in front. Pull the leaves in the center off to each side a bit, so that each leaf can be seen as much as possible. Have fun creating these, and allow your inner artist to guide you. When you're satisfied with each bouquet, use a twist tie or rubber band to hold the leaf stems together.

Place the leaf bundles between two large books or on a table under a large book until you're ready to wear the headdress. (You can also store the leaves this way overnight before bundling them, if you need to take the project in steps.) This will keep the leaves from drying out and curling, and slow the fading process.

When you're ready to put on your leaf crown, set the bundles out and gather your hair clips and bobby pins. (Depending on the length and thickness of your hair, you may need more than one clip/pin for each leaf bundle.) Light a candle or two, if you'd like.

Charge the bundled leaves with words of gratitude for the trees you have worked with to create this delightful craft. You might say something like the following:

> *As the seasons turn, I thank you, trees,*
> *for allowing me to share in your beauty.*

Using a mirror to guide you, clip the first leaf bundle to the back of your head so that the leaves face forward and are mostly above the crown of your head. (If you have long hair, it works best to tie it in a low ponytail at the back of your neck first.) Now clip a bundle to either side of the first one, so that the leaves fan out and no space is visible between them. Clip the remaining bundles on each side of your head, lying flat on the top of your head, or wherever else they fit best, in order to create the image of the Green Man/Woman. Use hair clips and bobby pins to secure any stray leaf stems (and bring more with you in case you need to make adjustments, especially if you're out on a windy night!).

When you're finished wearing the crown, you can use the leaf bundles as altar decorations for Mabon or Samhain, or just return them to the Earth.

WAND CRAFTING

MAKING A WAND FOR USE IN RITUAL AND MAGIC CAN BE A simple process or an elaborate affair, depending on your preferences. Some Witches like to have a finely polished branch with ornate carvings and crystals at the tip, while others feel more comfortable with something that could easily pass for a plain old twig. You may want to experiment for a while as you hone your wand-making skills. Gather several random small branches from the ground so you can try different options. For example, sand one branch and merely remove the bark from another. Then take turns holding each one in your dominant hand. Which one feels more powerful?

You can use the ritual outlined in "A Ritual for Harmless Harvesting" (pages 113–14) for obtaining a branch, using a boline in keeping with tradition. Or you can look for already fallen branches in the vicinity of the tree you wish to use. (If you want a wide selection to choose from, head out after a storm!) This is a good option for those who would like to try working with a few different types of trees to see which energies they resonate with most. You can also simply ask the Universe to bring you a perfect branch for your wand—if you do, you will likely find that a branch literally makes its way to your front door or suddenly appears in your path while you're out walking.

When it comes to length, it is said that wands traditionally run from the crook of your elbow to the end of your forefinger or middle finger. However, many people find this to be impractical and will go for something more in the range of 9 to 12 inches (23–30 cm).

This is another opportunity to experiment—try out a few different lengths with your practice sticks before making your decision. Thickness is also a matter of preference, and what you're comfortable with may depend on whether you want to hold the wand with your whole hand or just between your thumb and forefinger. Ideally, one end of the branch will be wider than the other so that the base of the wand is easily distinguishable from the tip. You may find a branch that already has such a shape, or you can shape it yourself by whittling one end down to a graceful point.

Sanding, carving symbols, and adding crystals or other ornamentations can make your wand a one-of-a-kind creation, but these steps are never strictly necessary. Most Witches at least remove the bark from their wands, but if leaving it on fits your style, then by all means do so.

No matter what degree of effort you put into it, however, it's important to approach the task with reverence and focus. Make a ritual of the process—light a candle, burn some incense or essential oils, or even cast a circle before beginning. When the wand is finished, be sure to consecrate it and charge it with your personal magical energy. You can also anoint it with magical oils; tree-based essential oils like cedar, pine, and juniper are particularly appropriate.

Finally, be sure to spend time with your new wand, as it usually takes a while (some say years) before your connection with it can reach its full power. Hold it while meditating, use it to cast your ritual circle, keep it near your bed while you sleep, and even carry it with you when you're puttering around the house. The more you bond energetically with your wand, the stronger its alignment with your magical work will be.

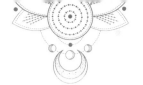

TREE INCENSE

MAKING INCENSE CAN BE A COMPLEX AFFAIR, DEPENDING ON the style you want to make (cone, stick or wand, or loose) and how many ingredients you want to include. Typically, incense blends involve some tree-based ingredients as well as herbs, resins, and/or essential oils. However, a single-ingredient incense also works well as an adjunct to ritual and spellwork. Below are a few single-tree incenses that require charcoal in order to ignite. (All of these can also be used in blends.) You can find plenty of instructions for making all kinds of incense online and in print sources (such as Scott Cunningham's *Complete Book of Incense, Oils, and Brews*).

BIRCH: Burn the bark for purification, especially after illness.

CEDAR: Burn cedar smudge wands or loose cedar bark chips to purify and consecrate sacred space.

FIR: Burn the needles to lift depression and clear out negative energy from a space.

OAK: Burn chips of oak bark for prosperity, or use it as a base for an incense blend.

PINE: Burn the needles for purification, for healing, and to attract money.

ROWAN: Burn dried leaves, bark, or berries for protection and to increase psychic awareness.

(*Note:* Always use a fireproof container for burning incense, keep water on hand, and don't leave burning matter unattended.)

AUTUMN HARVEST
EASY ABUNDANCE SPELL

THIS SPELL AFFIRMS THE ABUNDANCE OF THE NATURAL world via the gifts of the trees. It's an easy spell in that it calls for only what Nature has already laid out for you (which, in autumn, is plenty). Take a wander through the woods, your yard, or a nearby park and gather your ingredients while enjoying the refreshing air of the season. You might try incorporating this ritual into your Mabon and/or Samhain celebrations.

⸻ YOU WILL NEED ⸻

1 work candle for atmosphere

At least seven items from the following
(include as many of the trees as possible):

Ash seed pods

Pine, cedar, and/or fir cones
(or any cones from conifers)

Maple seeds
(samaras, also known as helicopters)

Acorns

Oak leaves

Holly berries

Any wildflowers still in bloom
(fresh cut in a vase or dried petals)

A wand

Light the candle. Spread the items from your harvest out on the altar in a visually pleasing arrangement. (Enjoy being creative with this step!) When you're satisfied with your work, pick up your wand and gently touch each item as you say the following (or similar) words:

As life flows through and from the trees.
Easy abundance flows through me

When you've touched the wand to all of the gifts, draw a pentacle over the altar and close the spell with the following (or similar) words:

I bask in the ease and energy of abundance.
Blessed be.

Leave the arrangement on the altar overnight, or for as long as you continue to feel fresh magical energy from it. The following day, or once you detect that the spell's energy is beginning to fade from the items, choose one acorn or cone to keep on your altar or carry with you. Return the rest of the arrangement to the Earth, in affirmation of your part in the natural flow of abundance.

WARM HEALTHY WINTER HEARTH SPELL

ENJOY THE QUIET AND RESTFUL ENERGIES OF WINTER IN GOOD health and warm surroundings with this bundle charm. It's ideal to work this spell in front of an actual fire, so if you have a firepit or an indoor fireplace, take advantage of it. However, you can create the semblance of a fire with several candles of varying sizes and heights burning close to each other (be careful not to let the flames touch each other).

Gather the twigs on a sunny day (even if it's cold out). You can focus on just one tree type for this spell or incorporate two or more, according to your preferences and what's available in your area. Conifers are the traditional winter trees for this kind of working. Rowan and oak bring in further energies of protection, strength, and healing.

≡ YOU WILL NEED ≡

A bonfire, hearth fire, or several candles

11 (ideally already fallen) twigs from one or more of the following trees:

- Cedar
- Fir
- Pine
- Holly
- Rowan
- Oak

Approximately 3.5 feet (1 m) of strong ribbon, twine, or thin rope

Scissors

Light the fire (or candles) and sit facing the flames. Gather the twigs together in a neat bundle and bind them by wrapping one end of the ribbon around them once and tying a knot. Wrap the ribbon nine more times along the length of the bundle, and tie another knot at the other end. Cut away any excess ribbon. Hold the bundle in both hands and say the following (or similar) words:

Heat and light of fire, comfort of warmth and health
are with me all this winter long.
Blessed be.

Keep the bundle near your hearth or stove (or another focal point of warmth in your home). In the spring, unwind the ribbon and burn the twigs in a bonfire with a few words of gratitude for any and all good fortune you experienced over the winter, or sprinkle the twigs around the area where you got them.

"BUILD YOUR OWN" PROTECTION WITCH JAR

THIS WITCH JAR CAN BE AN ALL-PURPOSE PROTECTION SPELL, or it can be tailored to emphasize a specific need (chief protective uses are listed next to each ingredient). To incorporate the energies of sacred numbers, choose at least three but ideally seven or nine trees to work with.

Adjunct refers to ingredients that lend power to the other ingredients but are not particularly strong on their own for this purpose.

=== YOU WILL NEED ===

3, 7, or 9 of the following:

Ash bark and/or leaves (travel, especially on or near water, illness)

Holly leaves and/or twigs (bad luck, evil spirits, lightning)

Rowan leaves and/or twigs (negative energy)

Hawthorn (negative energy, lightning)

Birch bark and/or twigs (negative energy, psychic attack)

Dried slippery elm bark (malicious gossip)

Cedar leaves (general psychic protection)

Oak (general protection)

Pine (general protection)

Yew bark—use with caution, wear gloves (general, adjunct)

Fir (general, adjunct)
Dried coneflower petals (protection from illness)
Dried foxglove petals (unwanted spirit communication)
Dried geranium petals (negative energy)
Dried snapdragon petals (general protection)
Dried violet petals (negative energy)
Mortar and pestle
A small wide-mouthed glass jar with lid
A medium-to-large jar of maple syrup (or honey)
1 black or white spell candle

≡ INSTRUCTIONS ≡

With your fingers, break each ingredient into small enough pieces to mix together. Add the ingredients one by one to the mortar. Stir the mixture five times sunwise (clockwise) with the pestle. As you do so, visualize yourself and your home and family (if applicable) protected by a shield of white light.

Pour the mixture into the jar, and then pour the maple syrup over it to cover all the ingredients. Close the jar and set the candle on top. Light the candle and let a few drops of the wax melt onto the center of the lid to form a small pool. Press the bottom of the candle into the melted wax and hold it steady until the wax cools enough to keep the candle in place. Speak a few words relevant to your purpose, affirming that you (and your home and family, if applicable) are protected. Close your spell with "And so it is" (or similar words).

Leave the candle to burn all the way down. Keep the jar in a place relevant to your specific protective purpose, such as your home, car, or work space.

SPELL FOR WELCOMING LOVE
INTO YOUR HOME

THIS SPELL IS FOR BRINGING THE ENERGY OF LOVE INTO YOUR life. You can work it for romantic love, but it also applies to the love of family or new friends. It's about cultivating the experience of having love for others and allowing yourself to be loved. In fact, resonating with the vibrational frequency of any form of love will open up the pathways to bring other forms in as well.

═══ YOU WILL NEED ═══

Small chips of birch, willow, hawthorn, and/or elm bark

**Hawthorn flowers (if available and if working
for serious romantic love)**

Holly leaves and/or berries (optional)

**Fresh or dried buttercup, daffodil, honeysuckle,
and/or violet petals**

2 to 3 tablespoons of maple syrup

═══ INSTRUCTIONS ═══

Add the dry ingredients one by one to the mortar. Stir the mixture three times sunwise (clockwise) with the pestle. Spoon in the maple syrup (enough so that the consistency of the mixture is mostly liquid) and stir again three times. Spoon a tiny bit more syrup onto the index finger of your dominant hand and eat it. Then say the following (or similar) words:

Love is infinite and everywhere.
I now draw infinite love into my life.
So let it be.

Dig a small hole in your yard or in a pot of soil near your front door. Pour the mixture into the hole and cover it with soil. The spell will permeate the ground around your home, drawing the experience of love into your life.

"BACK TO NATURE" SPIRIT CHARM

FOR PEOPLE WHO LOVE BEING OUTDOORS AND CONNECTING
with the spiritual energies of the natural world, coming back
to "real life" can be a drag. This charm can help you keep some of
that high-vibrational natural energy with you in your daily life.

This version uses the traditional Celtic faerie triad, but feel
free to use a triad of any trees you resonate with personally. For
example, you might use birch, willow, and elm to emphasize the
energy of the Divine Feminine. Alternatively, gather shed bark,
berries, or cones from three different trees you encounter when
hiking or communing with Nature. Feel free to add dried wildflower petals, as well.

This work should be done outdoors from start to finish, but
if that isn't possible, at least take the finished charm outside to
charge it with Nature's energy while you speak your invocation.

≡ YOU WILL NEED ≡

1 work candle for atmosphere (optional)

**Shed bark and/or twigs from ash, oak, and hawthorn
(or trees of your choice)**

Dried wildflower petals (optional)

A small drawstring bag

Light the candle, if using. Lay out each piece of bark, twig, and so on in a circle around the drawstring bag. One at a time, starting at the top and working sunwise (clockwise), pick up each item and hold it between your palms. Close your eyes, breathe in, and visualize yourself suffused with the beautiful energy of places you love in Nature. Note any subtle energetic shifts that take place from your contact with this small piece of the tree. Give gratitude to the tree it came from, then add it to the bag. When you're finished, close the bag, hold it next to your heart, and say the following (or similar) words:

Spirits of the Earth and wood,
your light does me the greatest good.
Be with me as I make my way
through indoor spaces, day to day
until I'm free to roam again.
So let it be.

Keep the charm where you'll have ready access to it, in an indoor space you inhabit frequently (such as your desk drawer at work, or the room in your home you spend most of your time in). Get it out and hold it in your hands when you want to reconnect with the magical spiritual vibrations of Nature.

CONCLUSION

HOPEFULLY YOU HAVE GAINED FROM THESE PAGES A GREATER appreciation for the incredible magical energy of Nature. Ideally, whether you're on a hike, sitting in a park, or simply driving through the suburbs, you will never see the landscape around you quite the way you did before.

Working with trees and flowers is a uniquely rich form of magic, and it can be done anytime you're simply in their presence, even if there are other, nonmagical people around. A soft, intentional touch of your hand to a leaf or trunk is an opportunity to exchange energy with a magical being, with no one nearby even noticing. Communing with nature spirits can also happen on the sly, though you may want to avoid speaking to them out loud if you're in a public park!

As you continue to develop your practice and deepen your relationship with Nature, you may also want to incorporate natural magic into your life in new ways. Perhaps you'd like to study the Celtic Ogham, starting with the letters named for trees featured in this guide. Or you might learn one or more of the ancient runic systems and make your own set of runes from the branch of a tree growing near you. If you're blessed with property of your own, consider planting and tending a magical flower garden or sacred grove of trees that will grow well in your area.

Many Wiccans and other modern pagans passionately believe that we as a species need to work in harmony with Nature again, and this is a large part of what draws many to the Craft.

As a result, the practices of both covens and solitary Witches often incorporate working for the protection and healing of the

Earth, both magically and physically. You might volunteer to plant trees with an environmental organization or organize a river cleanup in your area, and set a magical intention for the work to have lasting impact. There are many ways to care for this planet of ours.

No matter where you go from here, may your path be blessed with the presence of beautiful, sheltering, abundant, magical Nature!

ACKNOWLEDGMENTS

THIS BOOK WOULD NOT HAVE BEEN POSSIBLE WITHOUT THE trees and spirits who spoke to me on the lakeshore since before I could talk, along with the infinite love and support of my family and friends. I am also indebted to the most magical black willow in the whole world (location undisclosed) for continuing to bless me every time I visit, and to the faeries on the island of Innishfree, for lessons in remembering old wisdom. To Shaun, for endless patience and enthusiasm for these projects. And as always, to Sally, the best lifelong karmic sister-friend a girl could ask for.

Working with the team at Union Square & Co. has been a life-changing experience. Thanks so much to Barbara Berger for her creative vision and insightful edits. To Elizabeth Lindy and Igor Satanovsky for another beautiful cover design; Christine Heun and Sharon Jacobs for the beautiful interior design, direction, and layout; photo editor Linda Liang for sourcing the artwork in these pages; project editor Hannah Reich; and production director Kevin Iwano.

SUGGESTIONS FOR FURTHER READING

WORKING WITH NATURE IN YOUR PRACTICE OF THE CRAFT is a lifelong journey, as there is no end to what trees, flowers, and other plant life can teach us about the inherent magic of the Universe. Here are just a few suggestions for expanding your knowledge of trees, flowers, and nature spirits. The identification guides included here cover all of North America, but there are also many guides for individual regions and even states, which may provide information on more species near you.

Tree and Flower Magic

Coulthard, Sally. *Floriography: The Myths, Magic, and Language of Flowers*. London: Quadrille Publishing, 2021.

Cunningham, Scott. *The Complete Book of Incense, Oils, and Brews*. Woodbury, MN: Llewellyn Publications, 2002.

Forest, Danu. *Celtic Tree Magic: Ogham Lore and Druid Mysteries*. Woodbury, MN: Llewellyn Publications, 2014.

Hageneder, Fred. *The Meaning of Trees*. San Francisco: Chronicle Books, 2005.

Hopman, Ellen Evert. *A Druid's Herbal of Sacred Tree Medicine*. Rochester, VT: Destiny Books, 2006.

MacLir, Alferian Gwydion. *Wandlore: The Art of Crafting the Ultimate Magical Tool*. Woodbury, MN: Llewellyn Publications, 2011.

Teague, Gypsey Elaine. *The Witch's Guide to Wands: A Complete Botanical, Magical, and Elemental Guide to Making, Choosing, and Using the Right Wand*. Newburyport, MA: Weiser Books, 2015.

Whitehurst, Tess. *The Magic of Flowers: A Guide to Their Metaphysical Uses and Properties*. Woodbury, MN: Llewellyn Publications, 2013.

Whitehurst, Tess. *The Magic of Trees: A Guide to Their Sacred Wisdom and Metaphysical Properties*. Woodbury, MN: Llewellyn Publications, 2017.

Tree and Flower Identification Guides

Brockman, C. Frank. *Trees of North America: A Guide to Field Identification, Revised and Updated.* New York: St. Martin's Press, 2002.

Crowder, Bland. *National Geographic Pocket Guide to Trees and Shrubs of North America.* Washington, DC: National Geographic, 2015.

Howell, Catherine H. *National Geographic Pocket Guide to Wildflowers of North America.* Washington, DC: National Geographic, 2014.

Rushforth, Keith. *National Geographic Field Guide to the Trees of North America: The Essential Identification Guide for Novice and Experts.* Washington, DC: National Geographic, 2006.

Nature Spirits

Andrews, Ted. *Enchantment of the Faerie Realm: Communicate with Nature Spirits and Elementals.* Woodbury, MN: Llewellyn Publications, 2002.

Forest, Danu. *Nature Spirits: Wyrd Lore and Wild Fey Magic.* New York: Wooden Books, 2008.

Pogacnik, Marko. *Nature Spirits and Elemental Beings: Working with the Intelligence of Nature.* Rochester, VT: Findhorn Press, 2010.

PICTURE CREDITS

ClipArt ETC: v middle, 16, 22, 24, 76, 80, 85, 86, 116, 130

DepositPhotos.com: © Zenina Asya: 87; © geraria: 99

Getty Images: *DigitalVisions Vectors:* bauhaus1000: 90; clu: 52, 58, 61; duncan1890: 39, 107; GeorgePeters: 2, 111, 122, 142; Grafissimo: 56, 64, 77, 83; ilbusca: v right, vii, 41, 44 right, 48, 62, 69, 89, 94, 100, 106, 108, 129 right; kate_sun: v left, 118, 125; mecaleha: 44 left; nastasic: 29, 68, 124 right, 131; powerofforever: 55; *E+:* NSA Digital Archive: 102; *iStock/Getty Images Plus:* Alhontess: 14, 75; graph_uvarov: 124 left; Andrew_Howe: 110; intueri: 129 left; Christine_Kohler: 93; gameover2012: 136; kotoffei: cover, throughout (stars); Oksana Kovaleva: 123; Little_Airplane: 67; NSA Digital Archive: 79; pikepicture: 127; Pimpay: 133; pleshko74: 72, 128; Ksenjii Purpisa: throughout (crescents, moons), iii; Nataliia Taranenko: 15; Ukkususha: 59; ULADZIMIR ZGURSKI: 13

Courtesy of Rijksmuseum: 33, 112

Shutterstock.com: Artur Balytskyi: 71, 74, 82; Croisy: cover (knot); Eugene Dudar: 35; Epine: cover (leaves, acorn), spine; mart: 63, 66; MitrushovaClipArt: 135; Morphart Creation: cover (bird), 11; NadezhdaShu: cover, throughout (pendant, radiating lines, crescents, lotus), 103; patrimonio designs ltd: 26; Vera Petruk: 31; Maryna Serohina: 113

Courtesy of Wikimedia Commons: ix, 18, 20, 46, 117; Josef Gikatilla: 8; Pearson Scott Foresman: 7

Courtesy of Yale Beinecke Rare Book & Manuscript Library: 5

INDEX

Note: Page numbers in bright green indicate summaries of plant characteristics, uses, and associations. Page numbers in *italics* indicate specific spells/rituals/crafts. Page numbers in parentheses indicate noncontiguous references.

A

Abundance, 8, 75, 78, 79, *124–25*
Acorns, 14, 78–79, *124–25*
Air Element, 5, 34
Air Element, trees and, 29, 30, 58, 61, 63, 66, 71, 79, 82
Air Elementals, 45–47
Angus Mac Og, 61
Animals, as messengers, 102
Animism
   defined, 3–4
   magical and spiritual significance of trees and, 6–9
   soul/spirit in inanimate objects, 4
   unseen force organizing/powering material world, 4
   Wiccan beliefs, 4–5
Apple wood, 16, 38
Apples, 14–15, 75
Aquarius, 85
Ariadne, 82
Arianrhod, 87
Aries, 58
Artemis, 63, 66, 68, 82, 87, 90
Ash, spells using, *124–25, 128–29, 132–33*
Ash tree, 18, 19, 21, 38, 56–58.
   See also Rowan (mountain ash) trees
Astral travel, 31, 34, 35, 58, 87, 90, 108, 110
Athame, 34
Autumn Harvest Easy Abundance Spell, *124–25*

B

"Back to Nature" Spirit Charm, *132–33*
Banbha, 90
Beltane, 14, 22, 27, 28, 37, 43, 44, 70, 83, 91

Berkanan, 21, 22, 60
Birch
   characteristics and uses, 59–61
   Druid uses, 12
   incense, *123*
   magical associations, 61
   as one of nine spiritual woods, 38
   rune names, 21, 22
   spells using, *128–29, 130–31*
Bonfire, 37–39
Brigid, 14, 61, 71
Brooms, 35–37, 56, 59
"Build Your Own" Witch Protection Jar, *128–29*
Buttercup flowers, 43, 96–97, *130–31*

C

Cancer, 68, 71, 82, 87
Capricorn, 68, 71, 82, 87
Cautionary note, 55
Cedar, 61–63, *123*, (*124–29*)
Ceres, 87
Cernunnos, 27, 79
Cerridwen, 61, 66, 87
Columbines, 43, 96–97
Common Wildflowers and Their Magical Associations (table), 96–99
Coneflowers, 95, 96–97
The Crone, 65, 66, 85, 90
Crown, Green Man/Woman leaf, *117–20*

D

Daffodils, 44, 95, 96–97
The Dagda, 61, 75
Daisies, 96–97
Danu, 66
Diana, 68, 79, 82, 87
Dionysus, 66, 82
Divination
   Druids and, 78, 83
   incense for, 84, *123*
   lilac for, 99

Divination (*continued*)
  for love, 15, 43–44, 90
  Ogham for, 12–13, 90
  runes for, 21–22, 84
  using trees for, 13, 63
  wands for, 14
Dowsing, 87, 89
Druids and Celtic magic, 10–16
  about: who the Celts and Druids were,
    10–11
  customs associated with trees, 11
  divination using trees, 13
  Graves, Robert and, 16
  magical traditions around trees, 12–16
  meaning of "Druid," 11
  mistletoe harvesting ritual, 11–12
  oak trees and, 11–12
  Ogham script/alphabet of, 12–13, 16, 134
  today, modern Druids (Neo-Druids)
    and, 15–16
  tree spirits, 12
  wands, tree woods and, 13–14
  wishing tree traditions, 15

≈ E ≈

Earth Element, 5
Earth Element, tree associations, 29, 30,
  63, 66, 68, 71, 76, 79, 82, 90
Earth Elementals, 45–47
Egypt and Egyptians, 31, 32, 63, 66
Elementals, 29, 45–47, 48
Elements. *See also specific elements*
  about: overview of, 5
  in action, trees as embodiments of,
    29–30
  Spirit/Akasha as unifying Element, 30
  wands representing, 33–34
Elm, 19, *64–66*, *128–29*, *130–31*
Enchanted Forest Meditation, *108–10*
Energies of nature
  animism and, 3–5
  being alert for changes in, 102
  connecting with nature spirits and,
    100–102
  today vs. the past, 3–4
  Wiccan beliefs, 4–5

≈ F ≈

Faerie triad, 56, 70. *See also* Ash
  references; Hawthorne; Oak
Faeries. *See also* Nature spirits
  about: definition of, 43
  brooms and, 35
  connecting with, 100–102
  dwelling places, 15
  Elementals and, 45–48
  flowers protecting cows from, 43
  flowers to break enchantments by, 43
  holly and, 73, 74
  protecting child from being kidnapped
    by, 59
  rowan and, 82, 83, 84
Fir, *66–68*, (*123–27*), *129*
Fire Element, 5, 34
Fire Element, trees and, 29–30, 58, 61, 63,
  74, 82, 85
Fire Elementals, 45
Fire, ritual
  bonfires, 37–39
  fireplace for, 38
  firewood for, 38–39
  warm healthy winter hearth spell, *126–27*
Flora, 71
Flowers
  folk beliefs about, 43–44
  gathering and growing magical flowers,
    91–93
  magical associations for common
    wildflowers, 95–99
  magical energy of, 40–42
  for ritual and deity worship, 43
  seasons and, 42–43
  ways to incorporate into rituals, 44
Forest meditation, *108–10*
Foxglove, 43, *96–97*
Freya, 43, 61
Frigg, 58
Futhark, Elder, 20, 21

≈ G ≈

Gaia, 66
Gemini, 63

Genius loci, 47

Geraniums, 96–97, *129*

Germanic traditions, 17–22, 64, 78, 88, 89

God (or Horned God) of the Forest, 23, 25, 28

Gofannon, 74

Goibniu, 74

Graves, Robert, 16, 25

Green Man or Green Woman, 23, 26–28, 79

Green Man/Woman Leaf Crown, *117–20*

Grimoire, 107. *See also* Rituals, spells, and crafts

Grounding ritual, tree trunk, *115–16*

Growing and gathering magical flowers, 91–93

≈ H ≈

Harvesting from Nature, 11, 34, 72, 92, *111–12, 113–14*, 121

Harvesting from Trees for Magical Work, *111–12*

Hawthorne, 14, 15, 38, 69–71, (*128–33*)

Hazel trees, 12, 14, 34, 38

Hazelnuts, 14

Hebe, 85

Hecate, 66, 79, 87, 90

Hera, 71, 76, 86

Herne, 79, 85

Holly, 24–26, 38, 72–74, (*124–31*)

Holly King and Oak King, 24–26

Honeysuckle, 96–97, *130–31*

≈ I ≈

Incense, 44, *58, 65, 78, 81, 83, 84, 87, 122*, 123. *See also* Trees, incense

≈ J ≈

Jar (witch), for protection, *128–29*

Journeying, shamanic. *See also* Astral travel

Jupiter (god), 7, 58, 63, 79

Jupiter (planet), 63, 68, 76, 79, 82, 90

≈ K ≈

Kings, Oak King and Holly King, 24–26

Knife (athame), 34

≈ L ≈

Leaf crown, Green Man/Woman, *117–20*

Leo, 63, 74, 79

Libra, 76

Lilacs, 45, 98–99

Lir, 58

Litha, 23, 37, 44

Loki, 66

Love, spell for welcoming into your home, *130–31*

Lugh, 61, 74, 85

Luna, 87

≈ M ≈

Mabon (autumnal equinox), 25, 28, 117, *124–25*

Magic

animism and, 3–5

incorporating it into your life, 134–35

spells and rituals. *See* Rituals, spells, and crafts

Magical associations of trees

ash, 58

birch, 61

cedar, 63

common wildflowers, 95–99

elm, 66

fir, 68

hawthorn, 71

holly, 74

maple, 76

oak, 79

pine, 82

rowan (mountain ash), 85

willow, 87

yew, 90

Manannán, 58

Maple, 54, 74–76, 117, *124–25, 129, 130–31*

Marigolds, 45, 98–99

Mars (god), 58, 74

Mars (planet), 63, 71, 74, 79, 82
Medicinal and other uses of plants.
    See also Magical associations
    of trees
  about: cautionary note, 55
  ash, 57–58
  birch, 59–61
  cedar, 62–63
  elm, 65
  fir, 67–68
  hawthorn, 70–71
  holly, 72–74
  maple, 75–76
  oak, 78–79
  pine, 81
  rowan (mountain ash), 83–84
  willow, 86–87
  yew, 89–90
Meditation, enchanted forest, *108–10*
Mercury, 63, 66, 85
Minerva, 58, 87
Mistletoe, 11–12, 42, 78
Moon, 68, 76, 87
The Morrigan, 87, 90

N

Nature spirits. *See also* Faeries
  connecting with, 100–102
  earning trust of, 101
  Elementals, 29, 45–47, 48
  elm association with, 64–65
  genius loci or "spirit of place," 47
  names describing, 48
  perspective on humans, 47
Nature, watching, communing with,
    viii, 49
Neo-Druids, 15–16
Neptune, 58, 76
Norse mythology and magic/ritual,
    (17–21), 45, 73, 83–84, 90
Northern European tree worship
  about: overview of, 10
  Druids and. *See* Druids and Celtic
    magic
  Germanic traditions, 17–22, 64, 78,
    88, 89

O

Oak
  characteristics and uses, 77–79
  coin tree, 15
  Druid reverence for mistletoe and,
    11–12
  incense, *123*
  magical associations, 79
  mistletoe and, 11–12, 42, 78
  Oak King, Holly King and, 24–26
  rune name corresponding to, 21
  species of, 54, 77
  spells using, *(126–32)*
  wishing tree, 15
Odin, 18, 19, 21, 58, 66, 73, 90
Ogham script/alphabet, 12–13, 16, 134
Olwen, 71
Orpheus, 66, 85
Osiris, 66, 68

P

Pan, 79, 82, 85
Paracelsus, 47
Persephone, 63, 87, 90
Pine, 80–82, *(123–29)*. *See also* Fir
Pisces, 58, 66
Pluto, 68, 90
Poseidon, 58
Protection witch jar, *128–29*

R

Rainforest jasper, 63
Resources, additional, 139–40
Rhea, 79
Rhiannon, 87
Rituals, spells, and crafts
  about: grimoire for the great outdoors,
    107
  Autumn Harvest Easy Abundance
    Spell, *124–25*
  "Back to Nature" Spirit Charm, *132–33*
  "Build Your Own" Protection Witch
    Jar, *128–29*
  Enchanted Forest Meditation, *108–10*

Green Man/Woman leaf crown, *117–20*
Harvesting from Trees for Magical Work, harmlessly, *111–12, 113–14*
Ritual for Harmless Harvesting, 113–14
Spell for Welcoming Love into Your Home, *130–31*
Tree Incense, *123*
Tree Trunk Grounding Ritual, *115–16*
wand crafting, *121–22*
Warm Healthy Winter Hearth Spell, *126–27*
Rowan (mountain ash) trees, 13, 14, 21, 38, 82–84, *126–27, 128–29*
Runes, 18, 20–22, 34, 60, 84, 89, 90

═ S ═

Sagittarius, 61, 74
Salamanders, 45
Samhain, 14, 37, 60, 117, *124–25*
Saturn, 66, 74, 82, 90
Saturnalia, 73
Scorpio, 87, 97
Selene, 87
Snapdragons, 43, 98–99
Soul
   animism and, 3–5
   in inanimate objects, 4
   seat of, 63
Spell for Welcoming Love into Your Home, 130–31
Spirit/Akasha as unifying Element, 30
Spirit/Akasha Element, 30
Spirit charm, "back to nature," *132–33*
Spirits, nature. *See* Nature spirits
Staff carrier (*völva*), 19
Staffs, 19–20, 32, 84
Sun, tree associations, 58, 63, 79, 85
Sunflowers, 95, 98–99
Sylphs, 45–47

═ T ═

Taurus, 71
Thor, 58, 61, 73, 74, 83, 85
Tree of Life, 8, 9

Tree spirits
   hamadryads, 6–7
   people fearing, 8
   range of who they are, 7
Tree Trunk Grounding Ritual, *115–16*
Trees. *See also specific trees*
   about: cautionary note, 55; overview of thirteen magical trees, 54–55
   animism and, 3–5
   cutting down, 7–8
   deities turning into, 7
   dependence on, 6
   divination using, 13, 63
   Elements and, 29–30 (*See also specific elements*)
   feeling pain, 7
   fruits and nuts of, 14–15
   harvesting from, for magical work, harmlessly, *111–12, 113–14*
   incense from, 123
   magical and spiritual significance, 6–9
   "old religion" and, 6–9
   religions revering, 8, 9
   symbolic representations of, 8–9
   tools of Craft practice from, 30–31 (*See also* Bonfire; Brooms; Wands)
   wind communicating via, 102
   wishing, 15
Triple Goddess, 68

═ U ═

Uranus, 85

═ V ═

Venus (goddess), 61, 71
Venus (planet), 61
Violets, 43, 98–99, *129, 130–31*
Virgo, 63, 76
Visualization/meditation, *108–10*
Völur, 19

═ W ═

Wands, 31–34
   abundance spell using, *124–25*
   apple, 16

Wands (*continued*)
  ash, (56–58)
  birch, 14
  cedar, 63
  dowsing, for finding water, 87
  Druids and Celtic magic, 13–14
  elder, 14, 34
  as extension of spiritual energy of
    trees, 32–33
  hawthorn, 71
  hazel and rowan, 14, 34, 84
  linking, 33
  making, 34, *121–23*
  maple, 76
  materials used for, 32 (*See also* woods
    used for, Harvesting from Trees for
    Magical Work)
  Norse ritual and magic, 19–20
  pine, 81
  power of, will/intent and, 33
  purchasing, 34
  spirititual of trees and, 33
  staves/staffs and, 19–20, 32, 84
  traditions employing, 31–32
  Tree incense, *123*
  uses of, 13–14, 31, 33–34, 87
  willow, 87
  woods used for, 14, 16, 33, 56–57, 58
  yew, 14, 89–90
Water Element, 5, 36
Water Element, trees and, 29, 30, 58, 61,
    66, 71, 76, 79, 87, 90
Water Elementals, 45–47
Wheel of the Year, 23, 25, 28–29, 75
The White Goddess (Graves), 16, 25
Wiccan cosmology
  about: overview of, 23

  God (or Horned God) of the Forest and,
    23, 25, 28
  Green Man (or Green Woman), 23,
    26–28, 79
  Oak King and Holly King, 24–26
  Wheel of the Year, 23, 25, 28–29, 75
"The Wiccan Rede," 38
Wildflowers. *See* Flowers
Willow, 12, 14, 36, 38, 85–87, *130–31, 132–33*
Wind, communicating via trees, 102
Winter hearth spell, *126–27*
Wishing trees, 15
Wood. *See also specific wood/tree types*
  for bonfires, 37–39
  "nine sacred," 37–38
  for wands, 14, 16, 33, 56–57, 58
World Tree, 9, 17–19, 57
Wreaths, 43, 44, 60
Writing systems
  ancient Germanic, 20–21
  Ogham, 12–13, 16, 24
  runes, 18, 20–22, 34, 60, 84, 89, 90

⸺ Y ⸺

Yew, 12, 14, 18–19, 21, 88–90, 110, *128–29*
Yggdrasil, 17–19, 57
Yule celebrations, 22, 74
Yule log, 57, 58
Yule tree, 18, 68

⸺ Z ⸺

Zeus, 79
Zodiac, magical associations. *See specific
    zodiac sign*

ABOUT THE AUTHOR

LISA CHAMBERLAIN is the successful author of more than twenty books on Wicca and magic, including *Wicca Essential Oils, Wicca Year of Magic, Wicca Candle Magic, Wicca Crystal Magic, Wicca Herbal Magic, Wicca Book of Spells, Wicca for Beginners, Runes for Beginners,* and *Magic and the Law of Attraction.* As an intuitive empath, she has been exploring Wicca, magic, and other esoteric traditions since her teenage years. Her spiritual journey has included a traditional solitary Wiccan practice as well as more eclectic studies across a wide range of belief systems. Lisa's focus is on positive magic that promotes self-empowerment for the good of the whole.

You can find out more about her and her work at her website, wiccaliving.com

ABOUT THE AUTHOR

LISA CHAMBERLAIN is the successful author of more than twenty books on Wicca and magic, including *Wicca Essential Oils, Wicca Year of Magic, Wicca Candle Magic, Wicca Crystal Magic, Wicca Herbal Magic, Wicca Book of Spells, Wicca for Beginners, Runes for Beginners,* and *Magic and the Law of Attraction.* As an intuitive empath, she has been exploring Wicca, magic, and other esoteric traditions since her teenage years. Her spiritual journey has included a traditional solitary Wiccan practice as well as more eclectic studies across a wide range of belief systems. Lisa's focus is on positive magic that promotes self-empowerment for the good of the whole.

You can find out more about her and her work at her website, wiccaliving.com